M000227611

THE
JOURNEY
IS THE
DESTINATION

Finding a Full Life in the Midst of Empty Religion

JEREMY BROWN
Foreword by Greg Nettle

Send correspondence or edit suggestions to:

Journey Church
Attn: Jeremy Brown
55 Allen Woods Lane
Three Way, TN 38343
Jeremy@ourjourney.com

ISBN: 978-0-578-30611-7

Cover and interior design: Harrington Interactive Media (harringtoninteractive.com)

DEDICATION

I want to dedicate this book first to my wonderful wife of twenty-five years. She's not only tolerated but *encouraged and joined* me in too many adventures to list. To my three amazing girls (and my son-in-law)—you guys are some of what makes life amazing and encourage me to walk closer and closer with Jesus in hopes that you will fall in love with the same Jesus I did.

I dedicate this work to the elders, staff, and spouses of Journey Church—they sacrifice more than will ever be known to help people take their "next step" toward Jesus.

And to the people of Journey Church for whom this work was composed! Thank you (all) for your selfless sacrifice over these eleven years!

In addition to all the people above, I want to thank those of you who contributed edits to this effort. People in and around Journey Church and friends and colleagues across the country read, critiqued, and offered input into the project. While we ultimately had to take a more "professional" route, I can't thank you enough for investing your time and giving your input to make everything we can out of this resource!

CONTENTS

Foreword 7

Introduction 11

SECTION 1: BELIEVE

1. Don't Just Believe and Behave..........................15
2. Belief Determines Behavior.............................31
3. Faith Is More Than Empty Religion.........................47
4. Find Your Redemption Story 65

SECTION 2: BECOME

5. Geared for Growth: Core Competencies of a
   Growing Heart 79
6. Pursue Identity: Living in the True View
   of Yourself...93
7. Pursue God: Living the "with God" Life..................107
8. Pursue Truth: Living Through the Lens of Truth.....119
9. Pursue Authenticity: Living the Healed Life 131
10. Pursue Relationships: Living with
    Like-Minded People................................145

Conclusion: The Journey Is the Destination....................155

Notes 161

About the Author...169

FOREWORD

Greg Nettle, President of Stadia

There was a time in my life when I sat on the front porch of our home and thought to myself, *If this life that I'm living in Jesus is the life that I'm inviting others to share, then I must stop, because it is anything but rich and satisfying!*

That's a hard realization to come to—especially when you're the lead pastor of a local church. But truthfully, it was an even harder reality for me to accept simply because I had banked my entire life on this whole Jesus thing.

I had taught the words of Jesus:

> Come to me, all of you who are weary and carry heavy burdens, and I will give you rest. Take my yoke upon you. Let me teach you, because I am humble and gentle at heart, and you will find rest for your souls. For my yoke is easy to bear, and the burden I give you is light.[1]

But that certainly didn't describe the life I was living.

I was tired, worn out, close to burned out. I didn't know what real rest was. I spent a few minutes a day with Jesus but rarely took the time to walk with him. Unforced rhythms of grace? You've got to be kidding! I had a schedule. A full schedule. A demanding schedule. After all, I was making a difference for

God's kingdom! In short, I was doing a lot of the right things, but I wasn't becoming the right kind of person. I was far more concerned about my behavior (and achievements) than I was about simply living the life God desired for me to enjoy.

My guess is you have found yourself (or perhaps are finding yourself right now) in a similar position. Church has become just one more obligation. Finances are tight—no room for generosity. *A small group? You've got to be kidding! Share my faith with a neighbor or friend? Not happening.* But I'm glad those days are behind me. And my prayer is you will put them behind you as well.

Jesus said, "My purpose is to give [you] a rich and satisfying life."[2] That's the life I want. Isn't that the life you want as well? Rich and satisfying. Life to the full. The abundant life. More and better life than you ever dreamed of.

I wish we could snap our fingers and our lives would change. Changed from driven to guided. From rushed to unhurried. Pressured to relaxed. Purposeless to intentional. Shallow to deep.

The good news is it can happen! Not with a snap of the fingers but with an understanding of what it really means to find our lives in Jesus. With a clear plan of action that will result in a transformed life.

We're on this journey together. A journey given by God. A journey filled with purpose, impact, and deep meaning. But how we navigate this journey is up to us. It can be a journey that is frantic, fearful, and demoralizing, or it can be rich and satisfying. Seriously, the choice is ours.

Will we become fully whom God intends for us to be? Or will we behave as if, even though we have chosen to follow Jesus, God doesn't really have the power to transform our lives?

God assures us in 2 Corinthians 5:17, "Anyone who belongs to Christ has become a new person. The old life is gone; a new life has begun!" And in Philippians 1:6 we learn: "God, who began the good work within you, will continue his work until it is finally finished on the day when Christ Jesus returns."

But once again, the choice is yours. God will never force his life upon you. You simply must accept his plan and become who that plan calls you to be. Picking up this book is your first step. In the pages that follow, you will experience what it means to have a rich and satisfying life as well as how to attain it!

INTRODUCTION

I can still remember the pungent smell of the over-chlorinated pool. I can still taste the warm, sweet "cherry balls" that came from the vending machine after it had baked all afternoon in the hot Arkansas sun. I can still feel the panic of learning to swim . . . in the deep end!

I spent part of every summer with my grandparents in Jonesboro, Arkansas. It was an amazing time filled with fishing trips, learning to whittle, trips to the local magic shop (shout-out to the Golden Grotto—it's still open!), and most of all, the *best part*, adventures at the Elk Lodge pool with my cousins!

We always had a blast getting together, quickly hopping barefoot across the hot asphalt and jumping in and out of the pool all afternoon. It must have been just the break my grandma and aunt needed—a lifeguard to take care of us and a few minutes of peace for themselves!

During those summers, my swimming skills progressed . . . well, swimmingly. Each year, I developed more and more skills as I moved from the shallow end, away from the terror-filled death grip I had on the side of the pool, to the middle by the safety rope, and, ultimately, into the deep end of the pool.

But the moment that terrified me the most was standing half naked, knees bent as I trembled like I was freezing in the one-hundred-degree heat. But I wasn't the least bit cold. I was petrified as I stood on that diving board just a couple of feet above the water. The depth wasn't what scared me; I'd already been swimming there. The jump didn't have me shaking in my skin; after all, it was just a couple of feet. What frightened me was being able to see all of it from one place. From the perch of the diving board, I could see just how deep the water was in which I'd been swimming. I could almost feel just how far I was from the security of the safety rope. I could now tell that the lifeguard was just a teenage kid and wasn't paying attention to me since I wasn't a girl in a bikini!

But here's what I learned very quickly amidst the daunting pressure from the next people in line telling me, "Go already!" The diving board isn't a fun place to be; rather, it's a fun place to *have been*.

This book is a bit like a diving board. From here, you'll be able to see there is so much more to living than just breathing in and out on repeat. From here, you'll be able to begin to understand what Jesus meant when he promised a "rich and satisfying life" in John 10:10. From here, you'll be able to see the "more" for which you were created. God wants so much more for you than just religious observance, passive obedience, or lifeless existence! My hope is the pages of this book will give you a compelling perspective of the life God created for you—it's so much more than what you have been experiencing! Use these pages like a diving board—see what the fun is all about, and then dive in!

Enjoy!

— Jeremy Brown

SECTION 1

BELIEVE

1

DON'T JUST BELIEVE AND BEHAVE

I grew up in what I now think of as a "believe and behave church."[3] Now if you're anything like me, you have an immediate reaction to that statement. Maybe something along the lines of, *Aren't believing and behaving both very important things?* You're right to have that pushback. Stick with me for a minute. I promise we'll get back to that.

I grew up with a system of beliefs that went something like this: To go to heaven one day (either when I die or when Jesus comes back), I need to believe some very important information about Jesus. Specifically, there is a God who loves me so much he sent his Son to die for my sins. If I accept him, he will pay the penalty for my sins (eternity separated from God).

This reduced the gospel to a list of "minimum entrance requirements to cross over the bridge and get into heaven."[4] If I believed the right things, then God was required to let me into heaven when I died.

Once that was taken care of, my job as a Christian was to behave for the rest of my life. Do the right things (go to church, give, serve, etc.) and don't do the wrong things (kill people, have affairs, steal stuff, and—for the love of all things holy, right, and good—drink alcohol or dance!). Then, one day either I'll die or

Jesus will come back, and I'll hear, "Well done, my good and faithful servant."[5]

That may not be what anyone in my childhood meant to communicate, but it is exactly how I felt. For me growing up in church, the Christian life was reduced to a life of moral management. If that was true, what was all that business Jesus meant by his promise to give us a rich and satisfying life? But when I gave myself permission to be honest, I just didn't see it. I had a nagging question: *Is this as good as my life with Jesus will ever get?*

Fast forward from my childhood experiences fully immersed in church to my early forties in full-time ministry for over two decades. I spent most of my days at work trying to figure out ways to help people take their next step toward Jesus. When I got home, I spent the evenings with my wife trying to raise three wonderful young ladies. A little time with Jesus in the morning, work all day, and family in the evening—punctuated with a little downtime watching TV—and then I'd repeat it all the next day. If life with Jesus was just trying to manage my morality, I was getting a little bored. A far cry from a rich and satisfying life for sure!

BELIEVE AND BEHAVE

I'm a visual thinker. Most everything that bounces around between my ears comes out as some kind of sketch. If I were to sketch out the "believe and behave" picture, it would look something like this:

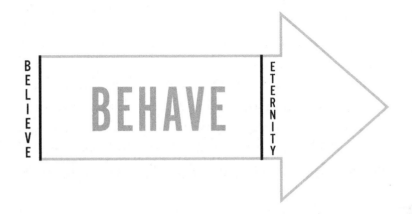

If we believe the right information about Jesus and mind our manners for the time we're here on earth, then one day we'll get to spend eternity in heaven where it won't be so much work to behave. That all sounds good except we can do all of that without ever having a relationship with Jesus.

Behavior is important and I would never want to diminish that (we'll talk more about that in the next chapter). But when behavior becomes the goal, we become outcome-focused rather than relationship-focused. We all know people—maybe even the one in the mirror—who have the right behavior but not much of a day-to-day walk with Jesus.

That's my story. For as long as I can remember growing up in church, as long as I looked the part, listened to the right music (and made sure I had just enough secular music around so I had something to burn when the time came to give up rock music again), made sure I was at church on a regular basis, and jumped through the right hoops, then all was well with my walk with God.

For all my experience in and around church and church people, I somehow managed to miss the value of walking with Jesus. The people around me valued knowing things about the Bible, the stories and the history around them, and the "deeper" meaning behind them. But what I missed completely was what those stories, the history, and the deeper meaning brought to me knowing the God of whom they spoke. Don't get me wrong. I'm certain the intent was there—I know that people intended for this to be a deep and personal walk with God, but while I learned a great deal *about* God, I somehow missed getting to *know* God.

It's entirely possible to do all the right things and completely miss a relationship with Jesus. What Matt Chandler calls "Moral Deism"[6] is the prevailing culture in the church today. Yet simply serving a God who wants me to behave and feel better about my behavior isn't all that there is! We were all made for more. Much, much more!

> It's entirely possible to do all the right things and completely miss a relationship with Jesus.

I invite you into "the more" that you were created for—a life not built around Jesus, but one that walks with him. Not a life of external behavior from an empty religious endeavor or a life of "[cleaning] the outside of the cup"[7] so nobody knows how dirty the inside is. I offer a journey *with* Jesus—a daily walk with him that transforms you from the inside out. Behavior is a crucial part of that picture, but it's the *result* of the journey rather than the goal.

BELIEVE-AND-BECOME FAITH

The purpose of this time that we have here is not to obey the rules and bide our time until that day when we get to go to heaven, but to use this time to walk with Jesus and become people who not only want to obey the rules but are also capable of ruling and reigning with Christ.[8]

Think about this for a moment. What if Jesus were to approach you today and offer you a new job? Except this job wasn't sitting behind a desk shuffling papers off to the next department or hanging shingles on houses; rather, this job was a formidable leadership role. Instead of offering some middle-management job, Jesus asked if you would give him a hand in ruling over the entire universe.

> Behavior is a result of the journey, not the goal.

As his representative, you'd have all the power and authority he has. Decision-making kind of authority. It may surprise you as much as it did me, but the core of the gospel is not your sin, but it's seeing Christ seated on the throne of creation. Ruling with him, you'd be responsible for endless power, authority, and riches. You'd have responsibility beyond the capability of your mind.

If you're anything like me, you'd be terrified! I'm not ready for that kind of responsibility! Most Christians probably think that when Christ returns and we're all with him in heaven, we'll be given new bodies and new minds, which will probably give us everything we need to be able to rule and reign with Christ, right?

To think that one day, when Christ returns, I'll go through some kind of "cosmic car wash"[9] where I'll suddenly be made whole makes me ask an important question: *What is the purpose of all the pain and experiences of this life?*

Here I am, a follower of Jesus for almost thirty years and more than twenty of those in full-time ministry, and this question still causes me to look deeper into what this whole relationship with Jesus is all about. Important and substantial questions haunt my mind. If God has me here on this earth for a purpose, then what is it? Why go through difficult times in this life when he's just going to wash it all clean and start over one day? What in this life ultimately matters in eternity? What value does growing in my relationship with Jesus today add to eternity?

You were made for more than just living and breathing.

> **YOU WERE MADE TO BE, WITH CHRIST, A CONQUEROR EXPERIENCING THE FREEDOM THAT HE CAME TO GIVE.**

You were made for more!

LIFE ISN'T ABOUT BEHAVING BUT BECOMING

This life is a training ground for a much more substantial mission: ruling and reigning with our Savior for all eternity. We need to stop looking at our belief in key tenets about Jesus as our admission ticket into heaven and our behavior as what we *should* do as payback for what he's done for us (what John Piper refers to as a "debtor's ethic"[10]). Instead, we need to understand the invitation to be the restoration of what we were created to be in the first place: people in a close, personal connection with our creator. God takes our belief as the first steps on a journey *with* him—a journey of becoming. Maybe that drawing should look a little more like this:

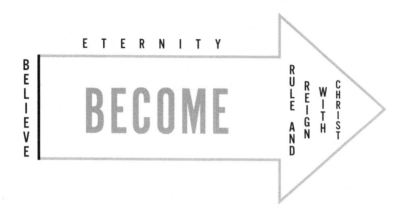

BELIEVING IS JUST THE BEGINNING

I remember exactly where I was when I became a Christian. It was November 29, 1989, and I was at Wheaton College to see DeGarmo and Key, a Christian rock band that had been black-listed by my "believe and behave" church (the opening act at that time was a completely unknown group of rap/singing artists known as DC Talk.) At some point during the show, with just the right amount of haze filling the air, Eddie DeGarmo, with the most amazing hair the '80s had ever known, said, "Of all the disciples, I like Peter the most. Because Peter was a bonehead." The world of my "believe and behave" background clashed with the reality that some people who followed Jesus still made dumb choices (maybe even most days in Peter's case). Even though Peter made some crazy choices (running off at the mouth, letting his actions get ahead of his brain—stuff I could easily identify with), Jesus still included Peter in his inner circle.

When Eddie then explained that God loved people like Peter so much that he gave his Son to die for their sins, I was floored. Not because I hadn't heard that before; after all, I had grown up in church. I had not only heard that before, but I also had responded to this kind of message countless times before. Evangelistic events, camps, conferences, campfires . . . they were all opportunities for me to try again with the hope that "maybe it would take this time."

Somehow this time was different for me. I determined to make this one the real deal, and I went forward at his invitation. When Eddie asked who had decided for the first time, I felt my hand go up. But it wasn't the first time I'd said these words. It wasn't the first time I'd gone forward. It wasn't the first time I'd done *any* of this. But it *was* the first time I truly committed to following Jesus beyond a decision (like Peter had done).

Up until that moment, I had viewed the mental assent to those facts about God (his love for me, sending his Son, etc.) as the "end" of the question rather than the beginning of a new life following Jesus.

In Matthew 4, Jesus walked up on a few guys fishing. They weren't just "wetting a hook" or goofing off on the water—they were at work. That tells us something about those guys.

In their culture, every Hebrew boy received an education in the same way . . . intensely. They memorized large portions of the Torah, the first five books of the Old Testament. In today's culture, it feels like people should get a badge of honor just for reading those books. Genesis is interesting, Exodus is fascinating, but you start to lose me at Numbers . . . Leviticus . . . and don't get me started on Deuteronomy.

But not these guys; it was different for them. They strove for something much bigger than just memorizing some words. They worked toward a calling. Teachers (rabbis) eventually chose the best of the best of these young men to become disciples.

Other teachers like Jesus also had disciples. Every rabbi chose disciples to follow him, which was a privilege and honor. In those days, it would have been like being chosen in the first round of the NBA draft! These young men were superstars of their culture.

But not these guys. Peter (yes, that Peter), James, and John were out fishing. Which tells us they hadn't been chosen by a rabbi; instead, these men were the leftovers, the B-team, the regular "everyday Joes" of their day. Have you ever felt like you weren't as significantly gifted as someone else? Like you want-ed to make a difference, but weren't sure you could? Well, I've got good news: that's exactly what those men thought about themselves!

When Jesus said, "Follow me, and I will make you fishers of men,"[11] they saw it as a huge privilege! No wonder they dropped their nets and did exactly what he said. They didn't need nets for the journey they were going to take!

If we're going to live the rich and satisfying life, we need to understand that believing in Jesus isn't the "get out of jail free" card we've likely been sold. It's not the "loyalty program" card that gets us into heaven. It's not the end of the journey; it's the very beginning.

Over the years, I've become a bit disenchanted with the idea of prompting people to "give their lives to Christ." I know that sounds heretical, and maybe it is. But we've all seen that idea reduced to a simple, one-time decision where someone somehow found the courage to raise their hand, walk an aisle, or get into some water. Something substantial gets lost in the translation. Jesus doesn't offer an agreement that obligates him to let us into heaven when we die. He invites us into a relationship with him that leads to our spending eternity with him, and this relationship begins today.

Don't get me wrong: I still believe every word of the profession of faith that I made on that cold November day. I still believe it's the most important decision I've ever made (or ever will make). It just wasn't the *last* important decision on my faith journey.

So where does that leave you? What is your faith story so far? Did you decide to follow Jesus for that one step or for all the steps you'll take? Did you give your eleven-year-old life to Jesus and just keep the rest for yourself? Are you depending on an agreement with Jesus that you made at one point in your life, or are you pursuing a relationship with him? That was the choice Jesus asked those men in the boat to make. He didn't give them some watered-down invitation to follow him to the beach. Rather, he invited them to be "covered in the dust of the Rabbi."[12] In other words, walking so closely with him that the dust he kicked up landed on them.

FIRST THINGS FIRST

Before I wrap this section up, let's settle something once and for all. If you haven't begun a relationship with Jesus, then this is where you need to start. Not where the journey ends, mind you, but where it begins.

Maybe this is the perfect time to put this book down and tell God what you're now *beginning* to understand. Just stop right now and pray something like this to God. The words aren't important. Your heart is what matters:

> *Jesus, it's not a surprise to you, but I've done a lot of things in my life that are less than what you want from—and for—me. I've tried to live in my own power instead of your power. I've tried to find life in any place but you. Right now, I declare that I'm beginning a journey with you. I'm turning away from my own independence and leaning into a relationship with you, which you made possible when you gave your life as payment for my sin. Today, I invite you not just into my life, but to walk alongside me as I grow to be more like you.*

ETERNITY IS NOW IN SESSION

Eternity is a hard idea to grasp because it's so long and seems so far away. If we're honest about it, eternity seems disconnected to our lives today. Eternity seems promising, exciting, and unfathomable, yet . . . irrelevant.

I can see the efforts of Satan, our collective enemy, at work here. Think about it: if he can somehow remove the relevance of eternity and replace it with what matters to us today (our marriages, our devices, our vices), then he can get our eyes off the prize.

But what if eternity wasn't some distant time and place disconnected from our lives? What if eternity was now? What if eternity was here? That would make it the most relevant thing we could consider, wouldn't it?

C. S. Lewis wrote *The Screwtape Letters,* which is a fictional series of letters between two demons: an older demon (Screwtape) and his young nephew (Wormwood). The book can be difficult to read because the word "enemy" doesn't refer to Satan, but rather to God (since they're fictional demons), but watch Screwtape's instructions as it pertains to eternity:

> The humans live in time but our Enemy destines them to eternity. He therefore, I believe, wants them to attend chiefly to two things, to eternity itself, and to that point of time which they call the Present. For the Present is the point at which time touches eternity. . . . He would therefore have them continually concerned either with eternity (which means being concerned with Him) or with the Present . . . or else obeying the present voice of conscience, bearing the present cross, receiving the present grace, giving thanks for the present pleasure.[13]

As Screwtape said, "For the Present is that point at which time touches eternity." Wow! Can you imagine the effectiveness if our enemy were able to disconnect our day-to-day lives from the whole of eternity? Losing that big picture would make today's very small picture feel very large. For example, if I were to experience discomfort today (the loss of a loved one, trauma, or a flat tire), then I would need to make today as comfortable as possible if today is all that matters.

What if I told you that God's plan was never for us to think of eternity as later but instead to think of eternity as now *and* later? When I was a kid, my parents didn't want me to have candy for several reasons. Some of the reasons were a concerted effort not to provide sugar to a hyperactive child, but they were also afraid that sticky candy would pull out my cavity fillings. One of those prohibited sticky candies was Now and Later. I'm not sure anyone really likes Now and Later candy—they are way too hard at the beginning and way too sticky at the end—but the name is profound. The customer is going to enjoy the candy now and want more later. What if that's what eternity is like? You get to experience some of it now—enough to make it relevant and real—but eternity makes you want more of it later!

So what are we to do *now* that makes us want more of eternity *later*? I don't know about you, but the idea of heaven has always sounded a bit on the boring side. I've always imagined it as the world's longest church service where we sing "Holy, Holy, Holy" for all of eternity. I figure something magical will happen to my attention span (and my ability to sit for long periods of time without finding something to occupy my rat's nest of a brain) between ending this life and starting the next one.

Don't get me wrong. I've dedicated much of my life to gathering people together for worship, but in the words of John Eldridge, "I like church as much as the next guy, but a weekend in Maui beats it hands down."[14] If we're going to get the full picture of what God has for us, we must have a better understanding of what God has for us in eternity . . . and it's much better than an eternal church service.

When the Navy SEALs, one of the most elite teams in America's military, train for battle, they don't train to play out every imaginable sequence of events—there are just too many variables. But they do train to make split-second decisions while keeping the highest priority on what ensures a mission's success.

That's your life right now! You're not in some waiting period where Christians anxiously await the return of Christ to make everything better. You're actively training (with live ammo) to become someone to rule and reign with Christ for all of eternity.

This life is a training ground. Every person who breathes air on this planet has a kingdom, a domain. You, and every person like you, have a domain. A car to maintain, a few bucks to ration out, a home to care for, maybe a marriage and a couple of kids. That is your domain, your kingdom. This period between belief and heaven is not a holding pen for believers; instead, it's a training ground for disciples.

The Scriptures refer to God as the "King of kings."[15] It's not just the idea that God is the King of King George and King Louis. The Scriptures are referring to you and me! We have a kingdom—possessions God gives us to steward to train us to be ready to rule and reign with him for eternity! This time isn't to be spent in neutral—it's to be spent in training!

THE JOURNEY IS THE DESTINATION

Understanding that today is part of the bigger picture of eternity changes what today is all about. Instead of looking to be comfortable today since I'm just biding time until eternity gets started, I face the reality that eternity ticks along, second by second, and I work to make a difference that resounds in the hallways of heaven!

About a year ago, our family faced a reality that almost every family with children faces at some point. Our three girls began the process of leaving home. Significant boyfriends at the time (one now a husband), looming college plans, and the beginning of the teenage years were among the life themes we watched unfold. For years, we'd taken an annual vacation where we typically lounged on the beach or went to a similar destination.

We realized our upcoming vacation would be the last all five of us would take together, which made this one somehow more surreal.

We wanted to make this vacation special. So instead of getting into the family minivan (a word I hope to stop using very soon!) and rushing somewhere like the beach or a city's skyline, we chose to undertake a very special journey. Some close friends of ours kindly loaned us their motorhome, complete with an onboard bathroom, large windows, and a separate bedroom. We planned an excursion unlike anything we'd ever undertaken before. The open road, the campgrounds, the crazy, off-beat attractions such as Cadillac Ranch, the WigWam Motel, Route 66, and a random corner in Winslow, Arizona, weren't the destinations: they were all part of the journey. Our destination wasn't a place out there somewhere; rather, our destination was getting back home. *The whole trip was a journey.*

Before we started the trip, we sat in our borrowed motorhome and clarified what we were doing. From this moment forward, we were on vacation. Our destination wasn't the Grand Canyon or any of the stops between here and there. Our destination was exactly where we sat this very moment: home. Every mile, every moment,

> The journey with Jesus is the destination.

every challenge, every scene would be a part of the journey back to this place. *The journey is the destination.*

That one perspective changed everything about the next eleven days. Instead of viewing that night's stop in a dark Walmart parking lot in Little Rock, Arkansas, as a necessary and uncomfortable evil of getting to our destination, it became part of the adventure. The break at the truck stop where we got

Makayla (our middle daughter who was about to graduate high school) to ask the clerk for "blinker fluid" wasn't a distraction from the monotony of the road—it was part of our vacation. (Yes, she fell for it. There's a link to the video in the endnotes![16]) The four hours we waited for a tow truck on the set of a Netflix movie in the middle of Oklahoma was frustrating, but it was part of the journey!

That's our lives with Jesus. If we redeem our view of eternity from a time that's almost completely irrelevant to our lives to understanding that this is God's intended place, we will understand that today's journey *with* Jesus is the destination.

The point isn't to get someplace out in the future where we arrive at the eternal beach or the eternal city's skyline. Rather, the adventure of today with Jesus is the destination we're shooting for! Sure, one day we'll return home for the rest of eternity. But let me ask this important question: If you don't enjoy the journey with Jesus today, what makes you think you'll enjoy it for the rest of eternity? Are you counting on something magical to happen that will somehow make you enjoy it, or are you learning to love time with him right now? God designed a life-giving relationship with him for you that isn't just about minding your manners until you stop breathing. What God dreams for you in your real, everyday life is the kind of relationship with him that brings real life to your everyday existence.

Father, I know now you designed my life to connect with more than just the days that I can count on a calendar. You designed my life to echo in the halls of heaven throughout eternity. I want to live for more than just today. Help me to live in the moment where today touches eternity. Amen.

2

BELIEF DETERMINES BEHAVIOR

You've probably heard, "Every action has an equal and opposite reaction." (That's Newton's third law of motion—who knew you knew something about physics, right?) If you were shooting a game of pool, you might be left with no other option but to bounce the cue ball off the bumper to hit your ball first. To do that, you would apply Newton's third law of motion (or just hit it and see what happens).

But over-action also produces an overreaction. If you hit the cue ball too hard against the bumper, it'll go flying off the bumper too hard, hitting not only your target but also a third of the other balls on the table and then sending them all rolling in seemingly random directions all over the table. The overly powerful action produces an overly powerful reaction.

I am a consummate over-reactor. My tendency is to take a stimulus and react so strongly that my reaction has little or nothing to do with the stimulus.

Here's an example: I told you I grew up in a church environment that put such a premium on my own behavior and simply believing that Jesus died for my sins (regardless of the motivation behind it) that these were the only tangible proofs of God's work in my life. If I did good things, I was a "good Christian," but if I wasn't able to keep it together, I was "backslidden."

At times, I have overreacted to that stimulus. To push back against the idea that belief and behavior were all that mattered, my default position was to think behavior didn't matter at all. Nothing could be further from the truth.

WHAT WE BELIEVE MATTERS

We live in a world that puts a high value on living "your truth." If you ask me, that's not only a risky venture, but it's a lie straight from the pits of hell. I know that is a strong statement given the cultural climate, but the world around us proposes that we get to define what is true for us separate from any kind of objective truth. That's dangerous ground to say the least. God, on the other hand, doesn't ask us just to live his truth as opposed to our own definition of truth—he offers us what is objectively true in the purest sense of the word.

To declare one view as objectively true innately declares that opposing views are false. To an unbelieving world, that sounds ridiculously *exclusive*, but God's declaration of objective truth is the most *inclusive* idea known to mankind. Here's why it's so inclusive: regardless of a person's background, race, socio-economic status, or culture, every person enters into a saving relationship with God through the exact same requirements—belief in God's objective truth. God doesn't lower the bar to accommodate a person's background or raise the bar because a person has resources—the bar of objective truth remains the same for everyone.

Not only is God remarkably inclusive, but he's also unbelievably kind and compassionate. Consider how difficult the idea of eternity, or life beyond the grave, would be if you had no assurances. You'd be left living with the hope you were good enough, faithful enough, or kind enough to make the cut. What kind of god would be so cruel to leave people working to achieve an unstated goal? God is not only inclusive of everyone by requiring the same standard, but he's also compassionate in explaining exactly what he requires for our redemption.

Not only is belief in God crucial to your salvation, but *what* you believe about him is equally crucial. For instance, believing God exists is important. But your beliefs *about* him, how he feels about you, and how to respond to him are all just as important as believing he exists.

This might initially sound unrelated, but if you were working on a 1973 Ford Pinto (arguably the worst car ever manufactured—we had one growing up that literally wouldn't start if it were raining), you would want to refer to resources closest to Ford Motor Company for information about how they designed the car. For the ultimate and final authority on objective truth, we turn to God's own words. After all, what he says about himself is the most dependable source on who he is—and what he requires of us to have a relationship with him.

If you've expressed a desire to have a relationship with God (maybe even as you read through the last chapter), securing the foundation of that relationship on his terms rather than your own is crucial. Probably the simplest way to work through these foundational beliefs is encompassed in the simple phrase "Jesus loves you." Those three words contain everything we need to base our faith journey on objective truth: what we believe about who Jesus is, how he feels about us, and what he requires of us.

JESUS LOVES YOU

To begin a relationship with God through his Son, Jesus, we need to begin with who Jesus is. If we simply ascribe the word or name "Jesus" to our own beliefs, we wind up believing in a person named Jesus rather than the one true Jesus, who is the Christ.

Let's start with the word "Christ." You might have heard Jesus referred to as Jesus Christ. If I'm honest, there was a time in my life where I just assumed that "Christ" was Jesus' last name. That's not what the word means. The word "Christ" means Jesus was the Messiah. The Hebrew people waited for generations for the coming Messiah—someone who would come save the people from their sin. Over time, that desire for a Messiah who would put an end to their regular sacrifices to make things right with God evolved into a hope that the Messiah would come to save them from the oppression of others—like us, they lost sight of the *true* hope of the Messiah. Christians believe that Jesus is that Messiah who came to earth as a man, not only to save us from our sin but also to give us that rich and satisfying life.

But Jesus wasn't *just* a man. Jesus is part of the Trinity. God the Father, God the Son, and God the Holy Spirit—all equally part of the triune God but also somehow equally individual. Simply put, it means Jesus is God—he's as much God as God the Father.

I know the whole idea of the Trinity gets a bit confusing, and I won't even pretend that everything we cover here will answer all your questions. It helps me to think of an electrical outlet. I don't need to understand everything about where power comes from, how the engineer wires or converts it, or how an outlet works to have confidence that when I plug my computer

34

into the outlet, it works. What you *do* need to understand is that the Trinity works, not necessarily *how* it works (yet).

There's a great passage in Scripture that demonstrates this whole idea for us. Just prior to his ascension back to heaven, Jesus said to his followers:

> Therefore go and make disciples of all nations, baptizing them *in the name of the Father and of the Son and of the Holy Spirit.*[17]

Plenty of other passages have Jesus saying similar ideas, but few as clear as this one where he clearly indicated his role as part of the Trinity. It's crucial as a follower of Jesus to clarify that we believe Jesus is God with skin. So if a person believes that Jesus exists, but doesn't believe that *Jesus is God*, we aren't talking about the same Jesus.[18]

Conversely, we can't believe in God in a generic sense and deny who Jesus is and still maintain the objective truth God declares about himself. Jesus declared clearly in John 14:6 that there is no way to the Father except through the Son. Check it out for yourself:

> Jesus told him, "I am the way, the truth, and the life. No one can come to the Father except through me."

It's just as important to recognize what Jesus didn't say as what he did say. Jesus didn't say, "I am a way;" rather, he intentionally chose the definite article "the" to claim he wasn't one option—he was the option. Remember, this is God's kind and inclusive love for us that offers every person entry into a saving relationship with him through the very same door regardless of who they are or where they come from.

What you believe about Jesus' identity is foundational to your faith in the life-giving Good News. Don't underestimate the value of what you believe about Jesus.

JESUS *LOVES* YOU

Now that we've established a solid foundation for who Jesus is, we need to talk about what Jesus came to do. There's no better person to ask about this than Jesus himself. There's an incredible interaction between Jesus and a tax collector named Zacchaeus in Luke 19. A tax collector was essentially a Jewish citizen who was a state-sanctioned thief. He was licensed by Rome to collect taxes from the Jewish people (and keep some for himself). One day, Jesus noticed Zacchaeus had climbed up a tree to see him. Instead of ostracizing Zacchaeus, Jesus identified him and went to his house for dinner that night. During this interaction, Zacchaeus came face-to-face with Jesus' identity and declared he was going to correct how he had wronged people. Jesus' next words were not only his response to Zacchaeus's revelation but a clear declaration of why Jesus came to earth as God with skin:

> For the Son of Man came to seek and save those who are lost.[19]

More than eighty times in the four Gospels, Jesus used the words "Son of Man" to refer to himself. [20] Judging from how often Jesus used those words, they were likely Jesus' favorite words to refer to himself. They carried much of the same weight as what we talked about in the previous section—he was declaring he was the Messiah. Next, he indicated exactly what the Messiah came to do: seek out and save the lost.

I've been working with people for more than two decades. In literally hundreds of conversations with people, I've never had to convince one person they had sinned. We all have parts of our story we wish we could do over, and we all have parts of our story we wish we could forget ever happened. But it's not enough for us just to realize we've done things that aren't right. We need to dive more deeply into whom we've sinned *against*.

This may not come as a surprise to you, but there's one substantial way you and I are not like God. You and I have the capacity to sin—a capacity we're all too familiar with. God, on the other hand, is holy. That doesn't just mean he hasn't sinned. It means God is completely "other" and has no capacity for sin.

When we walked away from God in sin, it broke something crucial in our relationship with him; we brought sin *between* us and God. God warned Adam and Eve that if they ate from the Tree of Knowledge of Good and Evil in the garden, they would surely die.[21]

Since God is holy, his character cannot tolerate or overlook our sin. Our sin is incompatible with God's holiness. To be made right with him, our sin demanded a substantial effort on God's part, something you and I have no capacity to offer. The word for this necessary payment is "atonement." Our sin against a holy God demanded payment.

That's where Jesus' love comes into play for us in the foundation of our faith. When I was a kid (probably like many kids who grew up in church), I heard John 3:16 commonly taught to children. Even if you didn't grow up in church, you've likely seen the verse on paper signs held up at football games:

> For this is how God loved the world: He gave his one and only Son, so that everyone who believes in him will not perish but have eternal life.

God is equally committed to all the facets of his character, which in this context refers to his holiness and his love. God's holiness demands payment for our sin, but his love offered that payment on our behalf. I love how A. W. Tozer spoke of the effect of the cross on our lives: "The cross is the lightning rod of grace that short-circuits God's wrath to Christ so that only the light of His love remains for believers."[22] Now *that* is a statement to summarize the foundation of our faith! God's wrath was justified because of his character, but the cross served to "short-circuit" his wrath to the Messiah, Jesus Christ, so we can see his unbelievable love for us!

To be able to substantially and faithfully build a foundation for your faith, you must believe in the Jesus who came to seek out and save the world through his unbelievable love for mankind. But to complete the whole picture, you must also believe he doesn't just love everyone—he loves *you*!

JESUS LOVES *YOU*

Faith is not corporate; it's personal. We've walked through the importance of believing the truth about Jesus' identity and what he came to do. Now it's time to bring it out of the ethereal and into our personal lives. Jesus didn't just come to save everyone: he came to save you. Saving you isn't just about keeping you out of hell; rather, it's about saving you from the dead-end life that sucks air in and out until we stop. Saving you is about giving you the rich and satisfying life that Jesus promised.

That means you and I must come to a personal realization of our own responsibility in our sin. It's easy to make attempts to justify our behavior by comparing our actions to the people around us. But remember, we're not obligated to just measure up to the character of the people around us—our offense isn't against them. Our offense is against God's holiness; thus, his character demands payment.

When I first started in ministry, I had a very difficult conversation with a lady. We had just finished a Good Friday service at our church. It was a powerful service where we had talked at length about the gruesome nature of the crucifixion. It was an intense time to say the least, which we concluded with communion in silence. The people who attended felt the gravity of their sin and God's love for us in the sacrifice on the cross.

The next week, this lady came to the office with an obvious weight on her face. She struggled to find words to express her dismay. She was upset—primarily with me. Her words will forever ring in my ears as the way that many people feel when they compare their lives to those around them. She said, "I just don't think anything I've ever done demanded anything like what Jesus did."

At first, I was offended. I thought, *How do you not see that your sin is such an affront to the character of God?* But as I considered her perspective, I realized she was saying the same thing many of us have felt. Essentially, she was saying, "Sure, I'm a sinner just like everyone else. I've done things that were wrong, but I'm not as bad as _____." But what she said wasn't as wrong as it was misguided. If we were to compare her sin to other people's sin, my own included, it wouldn't be that bad. But the conversations that followed helped her understand that

God didn't compare her sin to others. Instead, he compared her sin to his holiness, and that comparison demanded that Christ die in her place.

Atonement for our sin wasn't ascribed to settle "our" sin—it was ascribed to settle *my* sin against God. Romans 3:23 is such a simple verse, and it really helps me to understand my own responsibility.

> For everyone has sinned; we all fall short of God's glorious standard.

We're on equal footing when it comes to the fact that we've all done things that are wrong. We're all in the same boat together, but we must come to the personal understanding that we all still personally fall short of "God's glorious standard" (i.e., his holiness).

Here's what matters for you: We need to work toward building a foundation for our faith that isn't centered on our own behavior, but on the "glorious standard" of God's holiness that we *personally* walked away from. You and I are on equal footing. It doesn't matter how, when, or how far away we walked—the result is the same. I walked away from God to make life work without him, and that is an affront to the holy character of God, an affront for which I am personally responsible. God, in his infinite goodness and love, offered his Son as the ransom for my sin.

Jesus loves you. What *you* believe matters. The singular God of the universe, who expresses himself in three persons, the Father, the Son, and the Holy Spirit, loves you so much that he gave his own life to atone for your falling short of the "glorious standard" of his holiness. You and I receive the exact same opportunity to accept the free gift of salvation through the sacrifice of Jesus, the Messiah. He is, by his own declaration, the way, the truth, and the life. The sin that brought us to this point is not equal, but the cost of the sin is the same. It's on us to accept the personal responsibility for our sin and admit our personal need for his unending love.

HOW WE BEHAVE MATTERS

A few years back, I read *Save Me from Myself*, the autobiography of the lead guitarist for Korn, Brian "Head" Welch. The book details his childhood, the early days of the band, his struggles with meth addiction, and his life-changing experience with Jesus. I tell people jokingly that if you take the word "meth" out of the book, then the book would only be about six pages long.

The same is true of the Bible if you were to remove all the commands, encouragements, and directions related to behavior. Here are just a few:

And anyone who believes in God's Son has eternal life. Anyone who doesn't obey the Son will never experience eternal life but remains under God's angry judgment.

— John 3:36

If you love me, obey my commandments. . . . Those who accept my commandments and obey them are the ones who love me.

— John 14:15, 21

Work hard to show the results of your salvation, obeying God with deep reverence and fear.

— Philippians 2:12b

But don't just listen to God's word. You must do what it says. Otherwise, you are only fooling yourselves.

— James 1:22

What good is it, dear brothers and sisters, if you say you have faith but don't show it by your actions? Can that kind of faith save anyone? Suppose you see a brother or sister who has no food or clothing, and you say, "Good-bye and have a good day; stay warm and eat well"—but then you don't give that person any food or clothing. What good does that do? So you see, faith by itself isn't enough. Unless it produces good deeds, it is dead and useless. Now someone may argue, "Some people have faith; others have good deeds." But I say, "How can you show me your faith if you don't have good deeds? I will show you my faith by my good deeds."

— James 2:14–18

If someone claims, "I know God," but doesn't obey God's commandments, that person is a liar and is not living in the truth. But those who obey God's word truly show how completely they love him. That is how we know we are living in him.

— 1 John 2:4–5

We know we love God's children if we love God and obey his commandments.

— 1 John 5:2

It would not only be unjust but also dead wrong to ignore those directive statements. Behavior is a crucial component to the quality of your relationship with Jesus. The pendulum needs to swing away from only a "believe and behave" faith, but it doesn't need to abandon behavior altogether. As John Ortberg says, "Obedience—rightly understood—is what a saved life looks like from the inside."[23]

I am not a patient person. Don't get me wrong, I'm patient with my own issues—just not other people. It's something that I need to work on. When someone tells a story with too many details, I sometimes imagine myself holding my over-anxious alter ego back, covering his mouth, almost needing to tie him up to keep from yelling out, "Will you cut to the chase already?"

There's a deep part in all of us that is over-anxious to summarize—even when it comes to matters of faith. We want to follow Jesus, and the temptation is to say, "What do you want me to *do* already?" Rushing directly to external behavior without first talking about internal transformation misses the point entirely.

External behavior without internal transformation is empty religious expression. The religious leaders of Jesus' day had all the right behaviors without the internal heart transformation that Jesus came to bring. That's why Jesus referred to them as "whitewashed tombs—beautiful on the outside but filled on the inside with dead people's bones and all sorts of impurity."[24]

Think about the context of that statement for a moment. Jewish people who wanted to live by the law were not allowed even to touch things the law determined to be impure. But Jesus said people become impure because of the impure motivations of their hearts, even if they showcase the external behavior of avoiding impure objects.

Our proper behavior pleases God's heart, but it's not a way for us to make God pleased with us. Let me explain. We need to get something important straight: God is already pleased with you. You are his child, adopted, and grafted into his family.[25] You are a saint.[26] Because of the righteousness of Jesus imputed on you, you are made perfect in God's sight.[27] You cannot do a single thing to make God love you even a little more; conversely, you can't do a single thing to make God love you even a little less. You are perfectly loved. When we choose to behave in a way that is good, it pleases the heart of God. But don't mistake that for making God more pleased with you.

Consider it this way: I love Father's Day. It's not because I get a day to do whatever I want to do (although that's not too bad). I love Father's Day because all three of my girls cancel their other plans, intentionally spend time hanging out with me, and express their love for me. Their intentional sacrifice makes my heart glad. Last year, our youngest daughter, Myah, was invited by some friends to go to the beach over Father's Day weekend. She asked me if it was okay if she went, and of course I said it was completely okay. Why? Because her sacrifice on some other day would make me happy and her absence on that day would not make me love her even a little less. Our choice to honor God in our behavior pleases God's heart, but it doesn't make him more pleased with us.

What our good behavior does for our relationship with God is make room for him to work. When we obey the things that honor him out of a heart to follow him, it's an act of faith. When God has our *natural* act of faith, it makes room for him to add his *super*—the result is *supernatural*. Consider what happens when children obey their parents. They could obey out of obligation. Their obligatory obedience doesn't leave much room for mom or dad to teach them. After all, they're just obeying out of obligation. But when the child chooses to obey out of an effort to love and honor mom and dad, their behavior leaves room for mom and dad to teach them greater lessons far beyond their obedience.

Because behavior is nearly tangible, it's an easy target for our enemy. On one hand, he can get us to focus only on the external, hoop-jumping behavior by getting us to believe God will be more pleased with us if we do what he says to do. Sure, the enemy must allow us to do good things, but that's an easy trade-off given that he gets to undermine God's love for us. On the other hand, he can convince us that God loves us no matter what and that our behavior doesn't matter at all. Sure, he must play up the value of God's love, but he's confident that our behavior will bring shame, guilt, and condemnation, which will eventually lead us away from God's love.

Our obedience to God's commands is vital. But what's important to understand is that our behavior is an external expression of an internal change, and it's an action that makes room for God to work in our lives.

King Jesus, I don't want to overreact to the emptiness offered in religion and run away from the importance of obedience. I want to walk with you and become the kind of person who wants to obey. Help me to discover how you've wired me to relate to you and the world around me! Amen.

3

FAITH IS MORE THAN EMPTY RELIGION

You were made for more than breathing,
More than playing small and running scared.
You were made to walk in freedom,
To love and laugh, to find out why you're here.
Your name was known before the earth was
formed,
You were made for more.

— Ginny Owens, "Made for More"[28]

Have you ever sat in church and had the nagging idea that church was really boring? Maybe you sat with a little feeling of condemnation and thought, *If I were a better Christian, all of this would matter more to me.*

Or maybe it was while you served on a team at church. You didn't put much thought into it before you showed up, and you didn't think much about it afterward. But then a week or two later, someone said that serving on a team was a great "next step" for people, and you thought, *I'm serving on a team, and I honestly don't see a huge value in it.*

Or maybe it wasn't really at church where you began to experience the tension. You faced a choice that you knew was on a list of sins somewhere. Maybe it was a corner you really wanted to cut, but you knew it wasn't morally okay. Maybe it was a conversation with a coworker of the opposite sex; for just a moment, you felt alive, but you knew it was wrong, so you opted out (or didn't). All the while denying it seemed like the first time you had felt alive in years.

For religious reasons, you knew the right thing to do (go to church, serve on a team, not commit infidelity), but for reasons you can't explain, you really wanted to do what was wrong. That's exactly what religion *alone* will do for you.

Recently, I scrolled through Facebook and a friend had posted a picture of a façade house. It was just a shell with nothing inside. I was intrigued, so I looked façade houses up online.

Hundreds of houses like this exist that look like regular homes with windows, sidewalks, and shutters, but nobody lives inside. For example, I found a house in Brooklyn that looks just like any other house on its street: a beautiful, little, brownstone townhouse with an obvious affinity for Gothic stylings. But that's not what is behind the door. If you peek through the window, you won't see a couch and TV peering back at you. You'll see a dingy, poorly lit room, enshrined in pale-green paint, with a single exit door.

You see, in 1847 this home was built as a family residence. But when the city constructed the first underwater subway tunnel connecting Manhattan and Brooklyn in 1908, the city purchased the property and renovated it to be a ventilation point and secret subway exit. No one has lived inside the house for more than one hundred years. The outside of the brownstone is just a façade to keep the neighbors happy. After all, nobody wants to live next door to an exhaust station from the subway. The house looks great on the outside, but nobody's home.

That's a great picture of what empty religion, at its core, is all about: a great appearance on the outside that fits well into the moral surroundings. But it's just a façade, a fake exterior that hides the dirt inside.

> THIS MAY COME AS A SURPRISE TO YOU, BUT YOU WEREN'T CREATED EITHER FOR INDULGENCE OR FOR RELIGION. YOU WERE CREATED FOR RELATIONSHIP.

IT ALL BEGAN IN RELATIONSHIP

One of the first glimpses we get of the character of God is in Genesis 1:26:

> Then God said, "Let us make human beings in our image, to be like us. They will reign over the fish in the sea, the birds in the sky, the livestock, all the wild animals on the earth, and the small animals that scurry along the ground."

Look closely at the words "us" and "our." Those are relational words, and they expose something crucial about God. He was *in relationship* before he created us, and he created us in a relational context for a relational purpose.

The same is true with God the Father, the Son, and the Holy Spirit. God, in his three distinct persons, *is* in perfect relationship. God wants that perfect relationship for us—not from us. When God created us differently than all the other living creatures that walk the earth, he gave us the capacity for deep, enduring relationship. A relationship he intends to have with us!

THE EMPTINESS OF RELIGION

Empty religious expression is exactly the opposite of that kind of relationship. It's the empty observance of a list of rules and rituals simply for the purpose of doing the right thing (or not doing the wrong thing) to not upset a god who is somehow keeping score. Where's the relationship in that? Or maybe a better question is: What do we relate to in our empty religious efforts?

Please don't misunderstand. When I use the word "religion," I'm not talking about a particular style of worship. I'm not talking about liturgy, music, preaching style, or anything else in a worship service. I am talking about the purely external efforts we offer—devoid of any kind of heart transformation—in an effort to please God. We can relationally connect with God or observe empty religion with equal ease in any style of worship.

That kind of religion offers nothing in the way of relationship. When we're hurting, it offers nothing beyond the topical salve of making us feel better on the outside. When we're wounded by what we've done or what has been done to us, it offers nothing to "bind up our broken hearts" and has no power to declare the freedom of the captive.[29]

IT'S ALL ABOUT TRANSFORMATION

Empty religious observation is contrary to the heart of what God wants for us in transformation. It only offers us a cheap, knock-off version that has us modify our behavior in hopes that one day we'll be changed from the outside in.

Romans 12:2 says Christians should not "conform to the pattern of this world, but [instead] be transformed by the renewing of your mind."[30]

> **LIFE CHANGE DOESN'T HAPPEN BY THE OUTWARD OBSERVANCE OF BEHAVIOR MODIFICATION BUT BY THE INTIMATE WORK OF GOD AT THE LEVEL OF THE HUMAN HEART—THE DEEPEST AND TRUEST THING ABOUT YOU.**

Over the years, I've heard the words "Do not conform to the pattern of this world" used to tell people they should not look, dress, or act like the world around us. But we miss Paul's point entirely when we reduce this simply to behavior. We need to consider what Paul meant: a changed life. The world around us has no access to a resource for change that comes from within. It only has access to change that comes from the outside. Take a brief look at any self-help book. What you'll see, time and time again, is a model of changing the way you behave on the outside in hopes that it will make a lasting change on the inside. It's worth noting again that behavior is a vital part of walking with God, but any empty religious behavior is putting the cart before the proverbial horse. Behavior is a result of transformation, not the other way around.

Amid the global pandemic of 2020, a friend of mine from church came to realize something was desperately wrong with his leg. For some time, he'd experienced terrible pain when walking. After a visit to the doctor, he learned he'd somehow fractured his kneecap. After weeks of modified walking with a cane and limited movement, he still didn't get any better. Further visits to doctors revealed his leg wasn't healing because it wasn't getting sufficient blood flow. The ongoing problem in his leg was really a problem in his heart! He needed immediate triple bypass surgery. A whole other medical team was necessary to bring healing to his leg—and even more so to his life.

This is the story of our lives. God alone has access to work at the deepest and truest level of who we are as people. God alone can change the heart—a change that will make a difference in our behavior. But we'll never be able to make behavior travel to the depths of the heart.

As Ronald Heifietz says, "We have the technology to fix the heart, but not to change it."[31] Think for a minute about the miracles Jesus performed. Miracles such as changing water to wine (one of my favorites), healing the sick, making the lame to walk and the blind to see, or even raising the dead. What you *never* see in any of those miracles is Jesus changing a person's character. That's because changing someone's character requires a volitional action on the part of the person.

Whenever we talk about actions on our part, someone will inevitably say, "Grace has nothing to do with works." I couldn't agree, and still disagree, more. Grace cannot be earned of God; we can't do even one thing to merit God's grace for us. But on the other hand, God's grace is not opposed to our efforts. Even the time you're investing to read this book is an effort. Showing up at church is an effort. Serving on a team, spending time praying, walking through life with like-minded followers of Jesus—they're all efforts. You and I must put effort into our own character transformation. It won't happen *to us*, but it will, however, happen *with* and *within* us.

RELATIONSHIPS MATTER

Relationship with Jesus is the context in which anything valuable regarding our . . . well, relationship with Jesus happens. What we do matters dearly, and it's not an overstatement to say that it matters eternally. But it all needs to happen in the context of relationship *with* God. As we talked about before, we all approach this relationship differently.

Some of us relate to Jesus through information, others in relationship, and still others by the potential of internal change. What matters most is that all of it happens while we're living what I like to call the "with God" life. However we begin this journey naturally, what's most important is that we walk *with* Jesus on it.

For instance, if what comes naturally to you is obedience, that obedience needs to have a heart of pleasing and honoring God rather than a heart of appeasing him. For some people, something like church attendance can either be a holy effort with the right heart or an empty expression of effort to make God happy.

If we naturally gravitate toward relationships, while community is biblical and even crucial, those relationships with people can't be an end on their own. We need to ensure that the heart behind them goes deeper than just enjoying being around people. For some people, being involved in a small group talking about the Bible can be a blast, but it's important to set our sights on something more significant than just hanging out with people. We need to connect that time with something deep within our hearts.

If we naturally gravitate toward internal change or matters of the heart, it's crucial they aren't just popular psychology or freeing discussions about brokenness, pain, or trauma we've faced. Rather, they require a God-led delve into what's exposed in us and how God wants to bring healing.

In the end, we can modify our behavior, pursue relationships, and even have deep, revealing discussions of our stories but never engage Jesus in relationship. In that instance, what happens internally doesn't really matter as it would if Jesus guided us, walked with us, and transformed us.

So where does that leave you at this point in your journey? Take time to evaluate not only your starting point on this journey but also your motivation behind the progress you've made so far.

HOW DID IT GET SO FAR AWAY?

Much of what we know as Christianity today is riddled with pious religion, rampant consumerism, entertainment, ego-driven leadership, and empty knowledge—just to name a few! How did we get so far offtrack? If we're going to move forward as disciples, we need to know what caused us to lose sight of such an important piece of being followers of Jesus.

I have a confession: I love those shows on HGTV where people buy a house and flip it for a profit. Now, I love shiplap as much as the next guy, but it's not really the decorating that pulls me in. It's the demo! I love when they take out the sledgehammers and get a look at what's really going on with the house. When they look behind the drywall and under the floors, they're able to see what years of neglect, poor building and wiring, and pests have done to the house. Once they've got a good picture of what needs to be replaced or rewired, they're able to rebuild a stronger, more usable home for the soon-to-be homeowner.

We're not going to tear this down to the studs and rebuild, but it's important to get a picture of what's gone wrong so we can know how deeply we need to cut to get back to a rich and satisfying relationship with Jesus.

THIS WHOLE IDEA WASN'T WRITTEN IN OUR CULTURE

Suffice it to say, the culture of the first century (when the New Testament was written) wasn't in the West, and it wasn't in 2022. When we read Scripture, we try to relate to Jesus in translation. Whether we realize it or not (or do a good job of it or not), we translate the biblical culture to our own culture. Remember, the Scriptures weren't written in English, and they weren't written to an audience with our perspective of the world.

There is a "plethora" (a word I learned from a great '80s movie with Steve Martin and Martin Short, *The Three Amigos*) of circumstances that need to be translated to our culture, but here are a couple to consider:

DRIVING VS. WALKING

It's worth noting the people of the first century didn't get places by motorized transportation. They got there by "hoofing it," walking from place to place. That may not seem significant, but it goes a long way to helping us understand how they defined life as opposed to how we define it.

Everyday life took work. For us, when we want to go somewhere, we decide where we want to go, put the key in the ignition, and drive from point A to point B. For them, the distance between point A and point B was a journey, and each step was valuable.

We've lost sight of the value of the journey. For us, getting from one place to the next is just a matter of navigating the traffic, stoplights, and idiots on the road—it's just a means to an end. For them, each step was part of the overall experience; the journey was valued. That seemingly insignificant piece is crucial to us. Today, we only value the destination. We've got to retrain our minds to value the journey.

When Jesus told those guys in the boat to follow him, he invited them on the same adventure he invites all Christians: a journey of following him every single day, walking the "with God" life.

> THIS MAY BE A BIT BLUNT, BUT YOU WILL NEVER EXPERIENCE THE RICH AND SATISFYING LIFE THAT JESUS PROMISES IF YOUR ONLY OBJECTIVE IS TO ARRIVE IN HEAVEN ONE DAY.

The life Jesus offers is only found in the journey with him.

BEHAVE VS. BECOME

We've already covered this a bit, but it bears restating and more developing. After all, the purpose of this project is to help you take your next step in *becoming* the kind of person who walks with Jesus rather than the kind of person who obeys the rules out of obligation.

Significant tension existed in the first-century world. Much like today, different people groups understood the world they lived in differently. A well-known group of people who centered their lives every day on obeying the law were the Pharisees. Jesus, offering a journey of becoming, was at odds with them often.

These men, marked by their outward efforts to meet the requirements of the law, completely missed the idea of a transformative relationship with God. But in stark contrast, when Jesus invited those men to follow him, he offered them a journey of transformation.

Zero in on the words he used:

> "Come, follow me," Jesus said, "and I will make you fishers of men."[32]

When Jesus called the disciples, he used formative language, not religious language. In other words, Jesus said he would form the disciples (and not force them) into fishers of men. Those words are crucial to your journey with Jesus. The invitation of Jesus isn't to be obedient to the law; instead, he invites you to be formed into a person obedient to him.

Since day one at Journey Church, we've defined a disciple of Jesus in these terms (based entirely on that verse):

FOLLOW–FORMED–FAITHFUL.

A disciple of Jesus is a follower of Jesus who is formed in the image of Jesus and faithful to the mission of Jesus. That's it.

FOLLOW

The call to the men in the boat is the same call Jesus makes to each of us: "Follow me." It's a simple call when you consider it, isn't it? Like we talked about earlier, they were looking for this kind of calling! But when you consider what it cost, it's much more involved. To those men in the boat, the cost of following Jesus meant leaving everything they thought would sustain them for a life they knew little about. That is what following Jesus is all about! Leaving behind what we think will make us happy and trusting Jesus to offer everything we need.

When I've heard the gospel presented, it's often been about my sin and God's love for us. A simple recognition that I have done things that separated me from God's love and that he loved me enough to bridge the gap between my sin and his love. While that's not a bad place to start, realizing that's not the entire story is vital.

At the end of the day, sins are our efforts to make life work without any need for Jesus. Let me explain. We're all likely aware of a list of things that categorize as sins (premarital or extra-marital sex, lust, greed, envy, selfishness, drunkenness, etc.), but we are also aware that's not a complete list. We are left to apply that list of sins to our seemingly ever-increasing ability to find ways to sin.

For instance, we can apply the verse "Don't be drunk with wine, because that will ruin your life"[33] to our lives, which includes any number of ways to dull our senses and inhibitions. Anything from drugs or even Facebook can dull our senses and inhibitions. So where do we draw the line? Entire groups of Christians have been created on where we draw those lines. One group might center on a "none of that" approach while another might center on "moderation." Can you see how these approaches don't center on depending on Jesus for meaning in life, but on sin? One could argue their religious efforts are as sinful as the sin they're trying to avoid.

Jesus' invitation is to find life in him! Following Jesus *begins* with realizing that our sins separate us from God, but it doesn't *end* there! Following Jesus involves a relationship where we have the initial understanding that we have committed sins that separate us from God.[34] Those aren't just sins because they're on a list somewhere. They're sins because we've tried to find meaningful lives without him.

Churches often use big words to summarize big ideas. One of those words that gets confused a lot is the word "repent." The word simply means to "turn away." But when we think of repenting, we usually think of being sorry for what we've done.

While sorrow for what we've done is a starting point for repentance, it's not the whole picture. Repentance isn't just being sorry that we did (fill in the blank), and it doesn't mean just stopping (fill in the blank again). Repentance is understanding why what we did was wrong and living differently. Not just replacing that same behavior with a more acceptable behavior but choosing to "turn away" from that *perspective on life* and turning toward the better way—the rich and satisfying life that Jesus offers. A life that finds ultimate fulfillment in Jesus.

After more than thirty years in the music business, Alan Cross did a deep dive into the now-common phrase "sex, drugs, and rock and roll" to find the evolution of the phrase didn't start with the Blockheads song in 1977, but rather in a 1971 article in *The Spectator* that characterized the culture of adolescents at the time by that phrase.[35] You can certainly make the point that rock and roll isn't sinful (and I would agree), but as an example, let's say that you were into "sex, drugs, and rock and roll" and got saved at the age of seven. When you came face-to-face with the reality that you had done things God said were sinful, you repented of your involvement. So then instead of pursuing those wrong things, you started looking for something like church attendance to fill the void. Can you see how you can replace something that was on a list of "wrong" things with a list of "right" things and still completely miss out on finding intimacy with God?

That's where following matters. If we focus our repentance more on what motivates us, we will find the life Jesus promises us and not just a better, healthier place to be discouraged. Without our walk with him and the actions of his Holy Spirit within us, we can't identify those deeper longings. But by walking with him and listening to the Holy Spirit, we can identify the motivations behind our actions and pursue what he has for us.

When we reduce the idea of following Jesus to the idea of being saved, it reduces the journey with Jesus down to a moment in time rather than a life of pursuing him. The word "Christian" doesn't refer to a list of beliefs about Jesus. It means "follower of Jesus."

FORMED

It's easy to think of following Jesus as a separate thing from being formed in his image, like it's one act to follow him and a separate one to be changed by him. But the natural flow from those first steps of following Jesus is a promise of what that "following" life will produce in us. He promises that he will make us into something we're not. He will form us into his image. The journey with Jesus is what yields in us the outcome of obedience.

It's easy to view the idea of being formed in the image of Jesus as some spiritual skill development. As if there's an acquired skill of doing things that are on some kind of "approved" list in heaven and not doing things that are on an "unapproved" list. Remember, the invitation to follow Jesus isn't getting access to a morality manage-

> The journey with Jesus yields obedience.

ment club; rather, it's an invitation into a loving and developing relationship with him. As we walk in relationship with Jesus, we learn to become more like him. This book (and the Bible for that matter) is not centered on getting you simply to behave in a way that keeps the commands of the Bible. Instead, it's centered on your becoming the *kind* of person who obeys those commands.

The rest of our time together centers on the journey with Jesus that forms us into his image. Remember, obedience is not the goal of walking with Jesus—it's the outcome. This journey is one of change that comes from God's work on our heart making its way out to our behavior, not externally conforming to the external behavior that somehow changes our hearts one day. The journey *with* Jesus is what will produce obedience in us.

FAITHFUL

There's a great story in the often-overlooked book of Haggai. But you'll need a little backstory. Solomon, one of the greatest kings of Israel, built an amazing temple for the people to worship God. But in 587 BC King Nebuchadnezzar destroyed the temple and took Israel into captivity. After they spent seventy years in captivity, fifty thousand Israelites returned to Jerusalem to rebuild their temple. They immediately laid the temple's foundation and built the altar before they met some resistance. As a result of the opposition, they bailed on the construction for fourteen years.

To make a long story short, God sent the prophet Haggai to tell them to rebuild the temple:

> Now go up into the hills, bring down timber, and rebuild my house. Then I will take pleasure in it and be honored, says the LORD.[36]

God said three things: (1) "Go up into the hills;" (2) "bring down timber;" and (3) "rebuild my house." Sounds simple, right? Go, bring, rebuild. That sounds great, but it's not much of a building plan.

Here's where this meets your life: God calls you to *follow* (go up the mountain); to be *formed* (do the hard work of bringing down the timber); and to be *faithful* (build the temple). If you're anything like me, you're thinking, *I don't know how to do that! What about the building plan? Where should I put the first walls? How deep should I dig the footer for the wall?*

That's not unlike the idea of being faithful to the mission of Jesus. You might think, *I can see how to follow Jesus, and I can see how following him will form me, but what does it mean to be faithful to the mission of Jesus if I don't really know what that is?* To that, God says, "Go, gather, and build." The plans for the mission will be laid out for you as you *go* and *gather*.

But like he did with the Israel, God gives clarity for the journey—a map. To them, he gave instructions, and to us he gives direction: to them, he said, "Rebuild my house," and to us, he says, "Build my kingdom." Both are big-picture visions of what he has planned for us, but we still need more clarity before feeling confident that we're being faithful to the mission of Jesus.

Jesus reveals our mission along the way. Psalm 119:105 says,

Your word is a lamp for my feet, a light on my path.[37]

A light on your path only reaches as far as you've walked. You'll understand the path you can't see when you get there. Therein lies the beauty and power of relationship! As you walk the path with Jesus, you'll understand what he wants to do in and through you. When the Israelites committed to the work, they got another message from God through the prophet Haggai. This time, it wasn't more instructions; instead, it was assurance that God was with them! He gave them the same rich and satisfying life he offers us—the one with his presence firmly rooted in the center.

Your journey with Jesus isn't about empty religious observation or mindless obedience. Your journey with Jesus is an invitation of becoming. By walking with Jesus, you're formed into his image and are empowered to join in faithful obedience to his mission. In the next chapter, we'll talk about how God uses our past experiences to help form us in his image and lead us toward the rich and satisfying life that he's promised.

Jesus, I know my relationship with you is less about what you want "from me" and more about what you want "for me." I want to walk away from empty religious observance of things about you and walk toward your efforts to form me in your image. Help me to follow the direction of your Holy Spirit and the helpful encouragement of your Word. Amen.

4

FIND YOUR REDEMPTION STORY

I love Jesus. By that I don't just mean I love the idea of Jesus; I love the *person* of Jesus. I love how he was playful with his disciples. I love how he became righteously angry and cleaned the temple. I love how he pushed the buttons of the self-righteous leaders.

I also love how Jesus went back to his hometown, unrolled the scroll of Isaiah, and read what the Messiah would come and do:

> The Spirit of the LORD is upon me, for he has anointed me to bring Good News to the poor. He has sent me to proclaim that captives will be released, that the blind will see, that the oppressed will be set free, and that the time of the LORD's favor has come.[38]

Just a couple of verses later, he said, "The Scripture you've just heard has been fulfilled this very day!"[39] This completely enraged the religious leaders because he claimed to be the Messiah. Obviously, Jesus hadn't read *How to Win Friends and Influence People.* This statement also almost got him pushed off a cliff in Luke 4:28–30!

Jesus also elicited such a strong response because he proclaimed freedom for the oppressed. The religious leaders knew very well the overwhelming weight of the law held people captive and freedom was not found in the heartless observance of the law. Instead, freedom was found in the redemption of their lives, which the religious leaders could not offer.

What holds you captive? My guess is you can name a sin or two that you struggle with, but is that really what holds you back? Or is that behavior just the natural expression of what really holds you back?

A FEW EXAMPLES DEEPER IN THE STORY

Jennie grew up in a home where she was often told she wasn't beautiful. Feeling less than beautiful, she instinctively ran from guy to guy who told her she was beautiful. She knew, somewhere deep inside, they weren't saying that because she was beautiful, but because they wanted something sexual from her. You could say her promiscuity was the sin holding her back, but more likely the festering wound of her childhood fueled her pursuit of men. Freedom for Jennie wasn't found in being celibate but in allowing Jesus to heal where she had not grown past the declarations of her dad.

Jim grew up without a dad in the picture. A constant struggle to figure things out without someone to "father him" through those difficult times left him trying to prove he had what it took to succeed. As a result, Jim always felt "less than" the other guys, so he always had a chip on his shoulder. It showed up most often on a ballfield where he played like he had something to prove. He was uber-competitive to the point where it took almost nothing for him to wind up in a fight. You could say his anger held him back, but really it was the inner feeling to be the very best or he was completely worthless.

Jeremy grew up feeling like he was in the way all the time, whether it was running late, not having his homework done on time, or having coworkers always needing better results. Because of this nagging feeling, he often resorted to faking he was further along in a project than he really was or believing his lateness was someone else's fault. You could say his problem was procrastination, or you could realize he really needed to be set free from the captivity in which he lived. He needed a word from God that he was enough—that God's love for him wasn't based on Jeremy's goodness but on God's goodness. This realization may not seem life changing to you, but it was for me. (Oops, I guess I tipped my hand—I'm Jeremy).

The brokenness in your life today is often really an expression of unhealed pain in your story. Your ability to overcome the experiences and trauma that hold you captive aren't found simply in changing your behavior but in identifying the roots of that behavior and pursuing healing through Jesus.

> The brokenness in your life today is often really an expression of unhealed pain in your story.

YOU WERE CREATED, BUT YOU WERE NOT MADE

A lot is said today about "simple foods," which are foods with a limited number of ingredients. Strawberries are simple foods. They have only one ingredient: strawberries. A less simple food is a strawberry shake. It has milk, sugar, cream, a bunch of other stuff to make it sweet, and a few strawberries.

When God created mankind in Genesis 1:26, he said: "Let us make human beings in our image." God started with the primary ingredient out of which he created us: himself. That means we carry within us the image of God.

Genesis 2:7 says, "Then the LORD God formed the man from the dust of the ground. He breathed the breath of life into the man's nostrils, and the man became a living person." God added the second ingredient, dust, and then mixed the two. So he used the dust of the ground and the breath of his life.

Get that? God created you with two ingredients: the image of God and dust. The very nature of God is at the core of who you are . . . and dirt. The DNA of the infinite . . . and the definition of finite. God created you with two ingredients: his infinite matter and what doesn't matter!

> God created you with infinite matter and what doesn't matter!

But it's much easier in our "without God" lives to identify with what doesn't matter than to identify with the eternal matter that resides in each of us. For that reason, the voices declaring we're not beautiful, not valuable, or we're in the way are much easier to listen to than what God says is true of us. We'll cover this in more detail when we get to the chapter on authenticity, but what's important for us to understand right now is that we weren't made who we are today. Instead, we were developed into who we are today.

Every single rejection, exclusion, betrayal, disappointment, failure, and struggle has played a crucial part in forming who we are today and how we approach life. The same is true of every success and triumph we've experienced. We can't separate what we've been through from the person we've become any more than we can separate the ingredients in a cake once they've gone through the mixer—they each play a part in the whole. To tell us to behave better without dealing with the cause of our behavior is like telling a cake not to be sweet; its sweetness is part of the mixture and can't be removed. Maybe also one day those calories just won't be there. Man, I wish it worked like that!

FRUITS AND ROOTS

Our lives are the result of the experiences we've had until this point. How we live today is the fruit of what we've experienced. What we've experienced in our past results in the initial reactions we have in our day-to-day lives. Left unchecked, those initial reactions result in our typical behavior today.

Just like those stories of people's lives (including my own) were a result of what they experienced, we all live today out of the total of our experiences. We may be able to find a way past our pain, but it's impossible to make it through deeply traumatic circumstances and emerge from the other side unscathed. This makes our walk with Jesus so personal. It's not about simply living out a list of predetermined behaviors; identifying the origins of our brokenness is helpful. To do that, let's look at a few categories of where that mess comes from. This will help us better understand the roots that need healing, so the resulting poor behavior is cut off at the source and no longer has power over us.

THE BROKENNESS IN OUR LIVES GENERALLY COMES FROM ONE OF THREE SOURCES: THE THINGS WE'VE DONE, THE THINGS THAT HAVE BEEN DONE TO US, AND THE THINGS THAT ARE THE RESULT OF LIVING IN A BROKEN WORLD.

All our stories are riddled with times when we've chosen to live outside of God's very best for us. Each of those moments carries specific consequences. For instance, if you spent a lot of time medicating your pain with a chemical, that naturally takes a toll on your body. Some of the behaviors that you experience today are a result of the brokenness introduced into your story by what you've done.

A staggering statistic is that one in four people is a victim of sexual abuse. As a survivor of sexual abuse, it pains me even to consider how many people are "walking wounded," carrying the daily pain of that abuse. Some of the pain we've experienced isn't our fault but because of something done to us. We are still responsible for the behaviors we engage in, but they stem from figuring out ways to make life less painful.

Finally, it's important to realize the environment we live in is not healthy; in fact, many times it's toxic. Often, the pain we've experienced is the result of that toxic, broken culture. Over time, the way we've learned to communicate, medicate, or compensate for pieces of our story are taught to us by our surroundings. This is the result of living in a broken world.

Every part of your story is crucial to your journey forward. It's those very moments and feelings that hold you captive, and Jesus wants to walk with you to declare freedom from this captivity!

BUT DON'T YOU HAVE A RESPONSIBILITY TO BEHAVE?

What makes a journey with Jesus different from popular psychology is that we aren't the mindless results of our stories. We play an interactive part in it and, even more importantly, we have a relationship with God that can identify character flaws in us and help transform them!

Make no mistake, your story informs your behavior, but you have a personal responsibility for that behavior. Assuming that because you didn't directly cause your behavior it's not yours to change would be easy. Yes, your story explains your behavior, but it doesn't mean you're not responsible for it.

I also love the miracles of Jesus. Who wouldn't love to see a man who was blind since birth be miraculously given his sight? Or someone who was crippled be given the unbelievable gift of walking? Or see a party that was losing its wind be given a second breath because Jesus turned the water into wine? But if you were to survey all the miracles of Jesus, you'd see him heal any number of infirmities, but what you wouldn't see is even more telling. Jesus never healed anyone's character. That's because the transformation of a person's character isn't something that can be done *for* them; it must be done in cooperation *with* them.

When we respond to God's goodness by allowing him to speak directly to those wounded places in our stories, something amazing happens. God begins the process of healing *how* we think about the world, our lives, and the people around us. As we walk in this way of seeing God at work in healing us, we'll begin to see God transform our minds as more con-

> When God speaks to wounded places, something amazing happens.

nected with our bodies. After all, it was our bodies that experienced trauma—we've just found ways to disconnect our minds from what happened. That's how we don't think about it all the time. But when we begin to experience God's healing in the pain of our stories, we start to restore the connection between our bodies and our minds. When our bodies connect more wholly to our minds, the darkness of our habits come to light and our wills become more aligned with God's will.

IT TAKES EFFORT

Your will is at the core of who you are. With your will you make the decision on where you want to live, what you do for a living, or whom you want to date or marry. Your will is completely your own. But since your will is completely your own, it can easily be out of alignment with God's will. Because of your broken, "without God" life, your will can become enslaved to your mind and body.

The religious efforts of the enemy teach that if we just modify our behavior enough (stop doing wrong), we will see transformation of our wills. But all we change is our habitual performance into something that's more desirable, so we don't really feel the need to invite God into the inner workings of our minds. Our wills remain entirely unchanged, just beaten into submission.

The transformation God wants for you is another matter. God wants you to possess the rich and satisfying life he created for you. That kind of life takes profound effort on your part. Not only the effort of identifying the "roots" of your behavior but working with him to identify the specific times you believed the enemy's lies about you.

For instance, I remember one of the first times I felt like I was in the way. I was about eight years old, and I made my way to the hallway where my dad was carrying a large armful of clothes to the living room. What happened next wasn't any more sinister than any eight-year-old kid stepping into the path of a full-grown adult who couldn't see him. My dad stumbled a bit as he knocked me down. All he said was, "Get out of the way, J.D."

But the enemy added his own narrative to my dad's words. My spirit heard, "You're always in the way." My dad didn't mean to communicate *anything* like that to me. If I had asked him about it, he would have clarified that. But I didn't listen to my dad's words or what I knew to be true. Instead, I listened to the words of the enemy, and I agreed with him. Following that incident, the enemy worked to refortify that agreement repeatedly so many times that I had to dig deep to find the earliest roots—he's crafty that way. My transformation in that part of my life took effort. Through cooperating with Jesus and digging through my story, God gave me the strength and clarity to replace the lies of the enemy with the truth of what God says about me.

I love how Dallas Willard speaks to this important difference between my effort to earn God's love and my effort to participate with him in my transformation:

Grace is opposed to earning, but it is not opposed to effort. Earning is an attitude; effort is an action.

If this either strikes a nerve or leaves you with a lot of questions, don't stop now! The freedom you're looking for is available to you. The principles and ideas that follow won't scratch every itch, but they will introduce you to the path you'll want to follow!

REDEMPTION IS GOD'S WORK TO MOVE YOUR STORY FORWARD

I'm amazed at how complicated we make the idea of following Jesus sound in church. We use words that nobody uses and talk about lofty ideas that never seem to meet the reality of our day-to-day lives. "Redemption" can be one of those words. In church, we'll sing about redemption and throw the word around in sermons like it's something that has already happened—something that we have no real part of. But redemption is not just what Jesus did. It's what he wants to do. It's not something that just happens *to* us. Redemption is something that's happening *in* us today, not just something that happens *to* us when we go to heaven.

Think of it this way: redemption is God's action of making good on his promise to mend the broken parts of our lives. One very important piece of that story is God ultimately redeeming us from the sin that separates us from him, but that's not the whole story. God wants to be at work in your life redeeming—or doing his part to heal the brokenness that has become the operating system of our lives and move us toward the rich and satisfying life (here and now) he has promised us.

At Journey Church, we exist to "help people take their next step toward Jesus." That's what redemption is: working with God to move your story forward. God wants to do more than make you feel better about the broken parts of your story. He not only wants to declare your freedom from captivity, but he also wants you to *experience* that freedom! Finding healing is just the beginning. Living in freedom is what the rich and satisfying life is all about.

You were created for more than just living and dying—more than just breathing in and out on mindless repeat until you stop one day and move on to the next piece. God created you to participate with him in your redemption story. He's not looking for you to earn his love; however, he is not opposed to your participation and effort alongside the work of his Holy Spirit. Let's join God in the journey beyond only external, religious behavior into participation with him in the redemption of our hearts.

Loving Redeemer, I want more than just doing the right things in empty hope that you are pleased simply by my obedience. I want to experience more of you—the more that gives me the rich and satisfying life that you promised me! Lead me to the place where I can see you at work in my life and join you there. Amen.

SECTION 2

BECOME

5

GEARED FOR GROWTH: CORE COMPETENCIES OF A GROWING HEART

I'm fascinated by all things mechanical. I could get lost for hours watching *How It's Made* or any of my favorite YouTube channels featuring people like Mark Rober. These guys take difficult mechanical principles and make them easier for people like me to understand.

One of the things I've "nerded out" on understanding recently is how gears work. Consider what a pair of gears looks like:

GEAR 2   **GEAR 1**

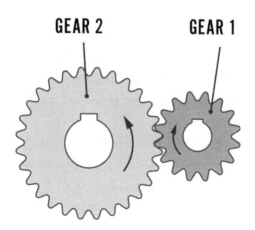

Each gear physically pairs with another gear to provide a specific, mechanical advantage. Together, the gears accomplish something that one of them alone could not do, such as increase torque, change speed, or even change the direction the gear turns entirely. It's fascinating if you ask me. But what's important here is that gears will help us understand something critical about our walk with God.

CORE COMPETENCIES

God uses several critical components, or you might think of them as core competencies, to deepen our walk with him. Consider that each category can house an infinite number of topics.

1. Pursue Identity: Living in the True View of Yourself
2. Pursue God: Living the "with God" Life
3. Pursue Truth: Living Through the Lens of Truth
4. Pursue Authenticity: Living the Healed Life
5. Pursue Relationships: Living with Like-Minded People

We'll cover all of this in more detail later, but to give you an idea of where we're headed, the category Pursue God: Living the "with God" Life includes skills like developing conversational intimacy with God, learning to hear God speak, and about a million other things.

The category Pursue Relationships: Living with Like-Minded People includes learning to become the kind of person with whom people want to journey, learning not to deprive other people of the benefit of you, and locking arms with them in the battle for your lives. You get the idea.

Each of those competencies works like gears; one gear by itself is completely useless, and two of them aren't as useful as when they're connected to other gears. And they're organized so if one is missing, the output is significantly affected or completely halted.

CONFUSION AND SIMPLICITY

The enemy works hard to make a real relationship with God *seem* unattainable. But developing categories like these allows us to navigate our walk with God without reducing the depth of what we're talking about. On the other hand, if you're not careful, you can easily oversimplify it and wind up with something that has no real-life value. An effective and growing walk with God is simple and real, but it's not simple.

Remember, Jesus came to heal our broken hearts and set us free from captivity,[40] not to educate or confuse us. Too often, Christian leaders try to sound profound or deep. What most people hear isn't profound but confusing. Remember, the journey *with* Jesus is the destination, and what we learn along the way is to serve that purpose—the "with God" life.

> An effective and growing walk with God is simple and real, but it's not simple.

I love what my friend Stuart Hall says, "The opposite of shallow is not deep. The opposite of shallow is personal. Personal will naturally become deep, but deep will struggle to become personal." Walking with Jesus rarely becomes deep until it becomes personal.

PROXIMITY CHANGES PERSPECTIVE

The year 2020 was encumbered with issues that have been immensely complicated. Infectious diseases, political strife, municipal mandates, political parties and perspectives, and racial injustice just to name a few. All those issues have complex underpinnings.

Back in early March of 2020, the idea of COVID-19 was a distant and complex subject. I didn't know anyone who had been affected. I routinely asked friends "Hey, you wanna hear a coronavirus joke? You probably won't get it." (Take a second for that to sink in).

Then in late March, I got news that my friend of almost twenty years, Stuart Hall, was not only sick with COVID-19 but also had suffered a heart attack and was on a ventilator. Suddenly, what was once remote and complex became very personal, and what became personal became very deep. Suddenly, I had an entirely different response to the conversations about ACE2 inhibitors and the availability of ventilators because that wasn't just "somebody." I had a face to put with the COVID-19 stories on the news.

The same thing is true about any topic: systemic racism, homosexuality, political perspectives, even the Bible and discipleship. The extent to which something becomes personally connected to your heart—the core of who you are—directly relates to the depth at which you'll understand it. Why? Because proximity changes perspective. The closer you get to something, the better you see it.[41]

So let's eat this in the living room. We're talking about our journey with Jesus and these five categories I mentioned before. What matters is not what you know about them or how you engage them, but how you walk with Jesus in them.

In his amazing book on developing the heart of a man, *Becoming a King*, Morgan Snyder says, "There is simply no substitute for intimate heart knowledge that comes through direct experience."[42] There is immense depth in these five pools, but they won't become deep to you until they become personal to you. You can't know how deep they go until you personally break the surface. Think of it like scuba diving: a friend can send you pictures from the bottom of the ocean, but you won't relate to how deep the water is until you join them on the descent. Whether it's diving or seeing the Grand Canyon, pictures and videos are nothing compared to seeing it for yourself. The full expanse of firsthand experiences cannot be conveyed until they are experienced.

But there's a barrier that can easily exist between knowing something as true information and the personal experience that makes it true in your day-to-day life. You've heard someone say knowledge is power. I think I heard it on a kids' program called *The Electric Company* on PBS when I was a kid. (I think I just dated myself, but friends don't tell friends that we're closer to 2050 than we are to 1990!)

Knowledge is the key to anything great. If I know a lot about a topic, I won't feel dumb in a conversation. Like many of you, I've had knowledge used as a weapon that deeply wounded me (and, ashamedly, I have used that weapon on others).

But knowledge isn't all good. As much as knowledge is a blessing, it can also be a curse. For instance, how often have we wished we didn't know something after the fact? We've all seen the man behind the curtain or how the proverbial sausage is made. One curse of knowledge is that we can't un-know what we know.

Another problem with knowledge is that you can't know what you don't know. I can't tell you how many times I've come to find out crucial information after I've already made a decision. In the words of the great twentieth-century philosopher Adam Sandler in *The Wedding Singer*, "Once again, things that could have been brought to my attention YESTERDAY!"[43]

But likely the most deceptive curse knowledge plays on us is luring us into believing that once we understand something, there is less now to be understood. We tend to look at knowledge like a pyramid that we work up from the bottom to the top. If we learn everything about a subject, in this case, discipleship, the Bible, or Jesus, then there is less to know. But particularly when it comes to matters of faith, that is a *gross* deception. A far more accurate understanding of knowledge comes to us when we invert the pyramid. Whenever we attain more knowledge, we discover there is infinitely more that we don't know.[44]

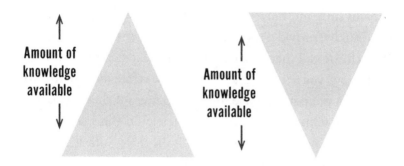

For followers of Jesus, this is where humility comes into play. It's so easy for us to hear something in church or read something in a book and stow it away as knowledge that puts us ahead of where we were (and, if we're honest, ahead of another person). We would rather do this than admit we are dipping our toes into the infinite and whatever we've come to know is simply an introduction into the reality of infinitely more that we don't know.

TWO KINDS OF GEARS

In any set of gears are essentially two kinds: the driver gear (the one using force) and the slave gear (the one receiving its force from another gear). Without getting into too much detail, your car works like this. The engine uses combustion (a series of well-timed explosions that occur as gasoline injects into a confined metal space that lights on fire and explodes as you press the gas pedal). The power from those explosions transfers into a drive shaft that leads into the transmission. The first gear to get power (the driver gear) transfers energy to a series of other slave gears, which then ultimately drive your car forward.

The same is true of your walk with God. Critical elements need to turn and move forward, but there must be a force that continually provides power. Within the context of Journey Church, we call that driving force our "next step toward Jesus." Right now, you're reading a resource that is intended to help you tap into a more sustainable source of power for those steps.

Many Christians depend completely on their churches to provide the power—or "next step"—in their walk with Jesus. This can be so detrimental to your walk with Jesus. Gathering with Christians is a critical part of your walk with him, but it cannot be the only source of power for the driver gear. If nothing else, church is only a couple of times a week. If your car only had one explosion every few days, it wouldn't make it very far. If you're going to sustain a consistently growing relationship with Jesus, you need to find a more sustainable source of power than just a gathering here and there to inject fuel into the confined space and fire to ignite the explosion.

A criticism I often hear from people who leave one church and head to another is, "I'm just not being fed." If I'm being honest (and hopefully not too harsh), that's very childish. Who else would say something like that? A toddler. In the book of Hebrews, the author talks about how difficult it is to explain the deeper issues of faith to someone who is spiritually immature. He uses the imagery of having to simplify the food down for people who aren't ready for the full meal.[45] For years, toddlers are dependent on the sustenance that comes from milk. But a time comes in the life of a child (and a follower of Christ) where they must consume food to sustain the systems of their body.

But how do we keep this drive going? What do we have that continually allows us to provide a driving force behind our walk with Jesus?

DISCONTENTMENT

Little in our lives has more power to drive us forward than discontentment. Think about it: When do you buy a new car? When the old one provides a level of discontentment. When do you change jobs? When the discontentment of your current job outweighs the comfort it provides. Discontentment moves us to action.

> Discontentment moves us to action.

I love movies. I love the stories they tell (and the fact that I can see it all in less than two hours). When Christmas comes around, we always watch a few classic Christmas movies: *Die Hard* (if you think that's not a Christmas movie, you're just wrong), *Christmas Vacation,* and *How the Grinch Stole Christmas.*

There's a scene in *How the Grinch Stole Christmas* when Jim Carrey (a comic genius) makes his way from the fictional town of Whoville up to the mountain he calls home through a pressure-propelled garbage chamber. Pushed through the chute by some unimaginable force intended for trash, he slams from Whoville up to the mountain, thrown harshly against the sides. He goes for loops, harsh turns, and eventually crashes into a pile of garbage. He complains that there must be a better way to do this. Discontentment.

We all experience discontentment in our lives. You've experienced it and so have I. Tensions within our marriages, conflicts with people, insecurity, that uneasy feeling in our gut that says, "There has to be a better way."

Our first inclination is usually just to change our circumstances. While that is sometimes a necessary part of moving forward, it's not always that simple. In fact, maybe the discontentment you feel—maybe even this very moment—could be a gentle, loving invitation from God to take the "next step" toward him.

Dallas Willard wrote a compelling work on the principle of the "divine discontent." This is hearing those moments of discontentment as a gentle invitation to explore deeper truths with Jesus. We all experience moments where life just doesn't measure up to our expectations. Our options are limited, particularly if we're not willing to let God work in them. Our divine discontent is simply choosing to see how God wants to use those moments to move us forward. Barring that, we're left only to see how the enemy wants to use them.

In John 4, Jesus happened on a woman retrieving water at a well. That's to be expected; after all, it was a well. But this woman's story was different. It was the time of day when other women of the community had already gotten their water and headed back home. She chose to get her water at a time when she could avoid seeing them. You see, she had a bit of a reputation.

When Jesus walked up to her, he asked for some water. She was thrown off because he was talking to a woman with a reputation (and a Samaritan woman at that). Jesus said if she knew to whom she was talking, she'd ask him for water because he had living water that would remove her thirst forever.

Now, this is where the story gets real for us. This woman was *super* discontent. She had looked for relief to her insecurities in many ways: different schedules for water pickup, heartless worship rituals, and illicit relationships with multiple men just to name a few. She had tried to answer her discontentment with every imaginable resource she had. But she hadn't investigated what the divine could offer her.

> ## THEREIN LIES THE DIFFERENCE BETWEEN BEING DISCONTENT AND OUR "DIVINE DISCONTENT"— WHERE WE TAKE OUR DISCONTENTMENT.

One of the best ways we can provide power to the driver gears in our lives is to take what the enemy offers as discontentment and turn it into the sustainable source of momentum for our lives!

Imagine what would happen if instead of waiting for Sunday to roll around, you listened intently to your heart for what nagged at you and made you feel uncomfortable. But instead of staying discontent, you leaned into it and, more importantly, walked with Jesus through it.

Those uneasy feelings likely expose a question in you that God wants to answer. It might be a question that you have about God's willingness (or, as you perceive it, a lack of it) to provide for you. What would happen if you were able to answer that nagging question? If you could take nagging questions to God and get dependable answers from him, you would have a sustainable source that continually outlined your "next step" toward Jesus! This source would be entirely customized to your day-to-day life and come directly from your loving Father who wants to walk with you.

THE FATHER ISSUE

The idea of a loving Father is difficult for many to stomach. The prevailing culture today is one of fatherlessness. So many people have difficult, non-existent, or even toxic relationships with their dads. Please do not let the enemy take away one of the most beautiful and vital resources God has for you.

Part of the reason we find it difficult to view God as a loving Father is because we view him through the lens of our earthly fathers. But we've got it backward. Our earthly fathers are not the lens through which we should see our heavenly Father. Our heavenly Father is the lens through which we should see our earthly fathers. This may be a source of discontentment to jump-start your journey forward.

FATHER IS A NOUN AND A VERB

Our dads weren't the first to the fathering game—God was. God intended fatherhood to be a loving relationship where children are taught to navigate the difficult roads of life. Many insecurities men have stem from not being fathered well by their dads. Conversely, many of the victories they experience come from being taught to navigate difficult circumstances at a young age.

I've learned much of this from people who had difficult relationships with their dads. That was not the case for me. My dad was always (and still is) a guiding voice in my life. But even though I had a positive role model, I still need to view my earthly father through the lens of my heavenly Father. Only then will I effectively be able to understand and forgive when my dad messes up. He is, after all, just like me . . . human.

Beginning the healing road of seeing our earthly fathers through the lens of our heavenly Father will not only induce compassion for the brokenness out of which our dads raised us, but it will allow us to experience the most valuable parts of our relationship with God: his desire to father us through these periods of discontentment. "Father" isn't just a noun referring to a person; it's a verb referring to a loving action. If we're able to identify where our hearts feel discontent, we're able to do two very important

> **"Father" isn't just a noun; it's a verb.**

things: interrupt one of the primary ways the enemy works to derail our movement forward and tap into a sustainable source to define our next step toward Jesus.

God is inviting you into deeper waters. No more empty religious actions—he's inviting you into a deeper, personal relationship with him. But that relationship won't become deep until it becomes personal. As your life meshes with the gear that is driven by his Holy Spirit, your rich and satisfying life begins. The bottom line is to move your life closer into relationship with him. After all, proximity changes perspective.

Life-changing God, at times you feel distant from me, but I realize that is not because you have moved, but because I have. I want to move closer in relationship to you. I don't want to "practice" my faith. I want to live it out from a place of close relationship with you. Help me deepen my relationship by walking closer with you rather than knowing more about you. Amen.

6

PURSUE IDENTITY: LIVING IN THE TRUE VIEW OF YOURSELF

I've heard just about every imaginable reason that a person might give for their reluctance to come to church. People have told me that lightning would strike or the walls would cave in. One guy told me the water in the baptistery would boil. (That one took some thought!) I've heard people say Sunday was their only day to sleep in, gas prices were too high, and both their ex-wives attended the church. But when people are honest about why they don't want to go to church, the most common reason is they're afraid they'll be judged by their past.

We all have parts of our stories that we wish we could edit or do over. And if we're honest, we're all afraid those regrettable moments could define who we are. Being defined by our biggest mistakes is one of the biggest fears we all have. But having someone else define you by your past is not the biggest tragedy. The biggest tragedy is when *you* choose to define yourself by your past.

> The biggest tragedy is defining yourself by your past.

How you view yourself has everything to do with how you live your life—you live out of your belief. Neil Anderson says,

"We cannot consistently behave in a way that is inconsistent with how we perceive ourselves."[46]

Let me illustrate. When Sheila and I got married in 1996, I was six feet tall and weighed a whopping 140 pounds if you put me in two pairs of jeans and soaked me down with a hose. I wasn't just thin; I was scrawny. Over the last twenty-five years, though, I steadily increased in weight . . . well, sometimes it was steady. As a result, not only did my weight increase but the way I viewed myself changed. I didn't slip into depression, but I subtly changed the way I looked at myself. When I saw an opportunity to eat junk food, I thought, *Well, what can it hurt? I'm already fat!* I believed the undesirable outcome had already happened, which led me to think eating whatever I wanted couldn't really hurt. The way I saw myself determined the way that I behaved.

About a year ago, I made some significant changes. I began by identifying the unhealthy relationship I had with junk food, particularly sugar. Then I started setting up some healthy boundaries when it came to eating (timing, sugar intake, etc.). But the biggest change came when I saw those first couple of pounds come off! Suddenly, I began to see myself differently. Instead of seeing myself as overweight, I began to see myself as a person investing in his weight loss. The result was amazing; the subtle shift in identity made a huge difference. When I was tempted with something that was loaded with sugar, instead of saying, "The damage is already done," I began thinking, *No, I'm making progress. There's no reason to trade what I'm accomplishing!* Do you see the subtle difference? It's not so subtle! The way I saw myself determined my behavior. Fifty pounds later, I'm still struggling to transition my thinking about who I am, but when I do, I continue to make progress.

What you believe determines how you behave. In fact, I would go one step further to say that you will never consistently out-behave your belief. The belief that you have serves as the foundation from which you live your life. My hope is for you to establish, and live from, a biblical view of yourself. When you define your-self how God defines you, you will see God at work and be able to respond to him.

> Establish, and live from, a biblical view of yourself.

But before we can really dive in to see what *walking with God* can do for you, we must talk about what *walking away from God* did to mankind. For that, we need to go all the way back to the beginning.

The first few chapters of Genesis are probably among the most familiar to people—maybe it's because they're in the front and the chapters people usually read before they stop reading through the Bible, or maybe it's because something is hardwired into humanity that yearns to know its origins. Either way, people are familiar with the story of Adam and Eve in the Garden of Eden.

But just to get us on the same page, let me quickly recap the story that's in Genesis 1–3. Adam and Eve were created by God's hand for a close and personal relationship with him. They were placed into a perfect creation that didn't have any of the under-pinnings of the fall that was soon to follow—no fear, no insecurity, no bad decisions. God said everything they could see was theirs to explore and enjoy. He only wanted them to stay away from one bad decision: eating the fruit that comes from the Tree of Knowledge of Good and Evil (Genesis 2:17).

God told Adam and Eve, "I want you to only know good. Explore it, enjoy it, rule over it. But there is also another option. You can choose to know the other side too, which is evil. But be warned, all the good things of this world will be forever tainted by even knowing about it. Please don't even know about it because it will kill you."

Of course, we know how the story progressed. Not just because we're familiar with the Genesis account, but because we've all lived it out in our everyday lives. We've all chosen to live in the knowledge of evil—we're all just as guilty as they were. But the moment they introduced sin into the perfect picture of the garden, they brought ruin to its beauty. In the short time that followed their choice to walk away, all that God had warned them occurred.

INSECURITY

Before we walked away from God, we were completely secure. Take a minute to imagine what that would feel like. It's hard to imagine, isn't it? Completely confident we had what it takes. Completely secure in our body image. Completely trusting, completely pain-free, completely . . . well, complete. That all changed the very moment mankind decided we didn't want to know just good, we wanted to know both good *and* evil. When we did this, insecurity entered the equation.

Look at what happened to Adam and Eve:

> At that moment their eyes were opened, and they suddenly felt shame at their nakedness. So they sewed fig leaves together to cover themselves.[47]

Their eyes were opened to the reality of their nakedness, and they felt shame at their nakedness. What was completely secure just moments ago immediately began to feel insecure. When we walked away from God, we began to feel the very same feelings that we all feel every single day: insecurity.

This wasn't God's punishing Adam and Eve for eating from the tree; rather, this was Adam and Eve's realizing all God said was true about knowing good *and* evil. They were paying the clearly outlined cost of knowing good *and* evil.

FEAR

Before that moment, Adam and Eve knew nothing of being afraid. No fear of rejection. No fear of betrayal. No fear of not having everything they needed. No fear.

Again, it's hard to even imagine what it would feel like to live without fear. We're so well accustomed to living in fear that it feels completely normal. We're afraid we won't have our needs met. We're afraid we'll be betrayed. We're afraid we'll be rejected. We can't even imagine what it would be like to live without that fear. But not Adam and Eve. Just moments prior they were supremely confident that they were safe in their relationship with God. But when they introduced sin into the picture, fear so completely overwhelmed them that they felt the need to hide.

For Adam and Eve, every day up to this point had been marked by time spent face-to-face with the God who had created them and sustained them. Now that they had changed the relationship outside of the bounds of what God designed for them, they had a feeling that could only be explained by a completely new concept for them: fear. Look at what happened when God came into the garden for his daily walk with them:

> When the cool evening breezes were blowing, the man and
> his wife heard the LORD God walking about in the garden.
> So they hid from the LORD God among the trees. Then
> the LORD God called to the man, "Where are you?" He
> replied, "I heard you walking in the garden, so I hid. I was
> afraid because I was naked."[48]

God already knew what had happened. He is, after all, God.
But imagine the sorrow in his heart when he heard his children
expressing a feeling he never wanted them to feel. They were telling him that they were afraid to see him because they weren't
wearing clothes—clothes that he never wanted them to need.

The very fear that we are so accustomed to was never intended to be in our vocabulary. We were never intended to feel it at
all. Yet fear entered the picture when we walked away from God.

SHAME

Before sin entered the picture, we never felt shame. But the
moment they walked away, Adam and Eve felt shame at their
nakedness (Genesis 3:7). We were never intended to feel shame.
I would initially say that it's hard to imagine living life without
feeling shame, but since the inception of social media, I've come
to realize that some people have no shame. But not only were
we never intended to feel shame, we were also never intended to
have anything to be ashamed of!

The moment that sin entered the picture, Adam and Eve felt
shame and began to *live* like they were ashamed—they began
to feel the need to blame someone else for their actions. Look at
their response:

"Who told you that you were naked?" the LORD God asked. "Have you eaten from the tree whose fruit I commanded you not to eat?" The man replied, "It was the woman you gave me who gave me the fruit, and I ate it."[49]

Much has been said and written about what happened between God's command not to eat the fruit of that tree and this moment. And honestly, much of it is true. Maybe it was Eve's fault for being deceived. Maybe it was Adam's fault for being passive. Maybe it was both of their faults for choosing to move forward. But the one thing that isn't up for argument is the result of their actions. They both felt shame—a feeling they were never intended to have.

We live every day with the feeling of shame hanging over us like a dark cloud. The feeling of regret for a decision or a series of them. The fear of being defined by our worst moments. The perilous feeling that we're a slave to our vice or addiction. The sheer terror of being "found out" and remembered not for who we are, but for what we've done or thought. Those are feelings that we were never intended to have.

Insecurity, fear, and shame were never intended to be a part of our vocabulary, but when sin entered the picture, they became not only a part of our vocabulary but the lens through which we see ourselves—they became our identity. They are the result of our walking away from God, which is a result he's been on a mission to redeem.

JESUS CAME TO CHANGE WHO YOU ARE

This is where the real story of who you are begins! As followers of Jesus, we are no longer identified by the insecurity, fear, and shame of our past. We are defined by God's amazing love for us! Jesus came to change who you are, not just where you go when you die.

So often, when we reduce God's amazing message of love to just resolving the "where we go when we die" question, we completely miss the most significant piece of the story! God didn't love you enough to send his only Son to pay the price for your sin just to save you from your sin and leave you in pain! The pain of insecurity, fear, and shame are vital parts of what God came to redeem in you.

ESTABLISH A BIBLICAL VIEW OF YOURSELF

For us even to be able to begin to live without insecurity, fear, and shame, we need to start by recognizing that those things were never intended to be the lens through which we view life. Instead, God has an entirely other plan for us. Rather than seeing life through the lens of our failures, we need to establish God's vision for us because of who we are in Christ!

Accepting Christ is far more substantial than we might recognize. When we think of the cross as just a way for us to go to heaven when we die, we miss the most amazing parts of the story. Paul addresses what happens to our story the moment we begin to follow Jesus in 2 Corinthians 5:17:

> This means that anyone who belongs to Christ has become a new person. The old life is gone; a new life has begun!

Let that sink in for a second. The old life of insecurity, fear, and shame is no longer your life! If Christ has entered the picture of your life, everything has changed. You are no longer defined by failure—that life is gone and has been replaced by a completely new life. This is the foundation from which you're intended to live. *You* are a new creation!

Beginning from that place of significance, we can establish an entirely new view of who we are, but this time it's based on our identity in Christ. That's the bigger story that God wants for us between now and when we spend eternity in heaven.

YOU ARE WELCOMED

When sin came into the picture, it brought insecurity with it.

> **BEFORE THE FALL, OUR GREATEST ASSET WAS BEING ACCEPTED, LOVED, AND WELCOMED BY GOD.**

After the fall, it became our greatest need. When we unify in relationship with Jesus, we are grafted back into the family of God—we are welcomed! We no longer *need* to feel the insecurity that surrounds us every day.

Our fear that we don't have what it takes can be answered by not only knowing that "he has created us anew in Christ Jesus, so we can do the good things he planned for us long ago,"[50] but by making sure that truth is installed deeply inside our hearts—in the same place the insecurity was.

Our fear that we won't have enough—that our needs won't be met—is replaced with the truth that my Father in heaven rules the whole world and cares for me and my needs. That's why Jesus told us this in the Gospel of Matthew:

That is why I tell you not to worry about everyday life—whether you have enough food and drink, or enough clothes to wear. Isn't life more than food, and your body more than clothing? Look at the birds. They don't plant or harvest or store food in barns, for your heavenly Father feeds them. And aren't you far more valuable to him than they are? [51]

Our fear that we're not smart enough, beautiful enough, or strong enough is answered by calling that the lie it is, rooting it out, and replacing it with the truth that we are God's masterpiece.

But that's not the end. Our sin separated us from being able to be with God. Because of the perfect sacrifice of Jesus:

- You're one of God's holy people.[52]
- You're one of God's adopted children.[53]
- You're given direct access to God through his Holy Spirit that lives in you.[54]

And that's just a few verses from the first two chapters of Ephesians! God's Word is packed with truths that apply to you. Learn them, install them, and firmly root them into your life. They are truer of you than any identity you could learn from your sin.

YOU ARE SAFE

But you aren't just welcomed—you are safe in Jesus. Your fear is unfounded once you identify with Christ.

Because of his sacrifice, you no longer face condemnation.[55]

> Because of his good work, everything will work together for good.[56]

> Because he came to you in your need, nothing can separate you from his amazing love.[57]

No longer do we need to be afraid of being honest with God. Because of our identity as sons and daughters of the Most High King, we are accepted without hesitation. Adam's terror and shame in the garden has been changed for us into reverence and honor. We no longer need to be afraid of God because we are loved and accepted by him. When we identify with Christ, we receive his power. Paul promises us this:

> For God has not given us a spirit of fear and timidity, but of power, love, and self-discipline.[58]

When we are afraid that we've wandered too far—afraid that we're no longer loved—we need to run to the foundation of our security in Christ and remember:

We know that God's children do not make a practice of sinning, for God's Son holds them securely, and the evil one cannot touch them.

— 1 John 5:18

So let us come boldly to the throne of our gracious God. There we will receive his mercy, and we will find grace to help us when we need it most.

— Hebrews 4:16

> But if we confess our sins to him, he is faithful and just to forgive us our sins and to cleanse us from all wickedness.
>
> — 1 John 1:9

YOU ARE SIGNIFICANT

When the new creation comes in and the old fades away (2 Cor. 5:17), significance replaces our shame. What was our place to cower behind the dumpster in fear of being disregarded and useless is replaced by confidence to stand in the throne room of the King of kings! Our identity in Christ gives us a role to play in the kingdom of God. Jesus himself said these things about you:

- You are the salt of the earth.[59]
- You are the light of the world.[60]
- Your good works cannot be hidden.[61]
- Your life will be fruitful if you remain close to him.[62]

Paul also writes:

- Your life is a work in progress that God will never abandon.[63]
- You are God's temple.[64]
- You are God's coworker.[65]
- You can do anything through Christ.[66]

Are you starting to see the bigger picture? And I haven't even scratched the surface! Your identity in Christ isn't just something that gives you a button that says you're a Christian, and it's not just a ticket to get into heaven when you die. Your relationship with Christ changes your nature at the core of who you are. Only God has access to change a person at the level of the heart, and that is exactly what happens the moment Christ enters the picture.

If you're going to walk with God, you need to begin by establishing a biblical view of who you are. Not by looking through the lens of your sin, but through the lens of Scripture that tells you who God says you are. Don't just agree with these truths. Don't just underline them in your Bible. Install them into your life. Identify where you believe the lies of insecurity, fear, and shame, and then replace them with the truths of your identity in Jesus.

In Deuteronomy 6:5–9, Moses intended for Israel to take the commandments God had given and apply them to their lives. We need to apply the very same principles of our God-given identity into our daily lives:

> And you must love the LORD your God with all your heart, all your soul, and all your strength. And you must commit yourselves wholeheartedly to these commands that I am giving you today. Repeat them again and again to your children. Talk about them when you are at home and when you are on the road, when you are going to bed and when you are getting up. Tie them to your hands and wear them on your forehead as reminders. Write them on the doorposts of your house and on your gates.

LIVE FROM THE BIBLICAL VIEW OF YOURSELF

You might remember our goal for this gear: to establish *and live out of* a biblical view of yourself. It's not enough to agree with good information, and while it's vital to know it and even memorize it, the most important part is to live out of it. In the next few chapters, we're going to identify four more gears that must keep moving to maintain a growing relationship with God. We didn't design these ideas, we just identified them in a way that makes it possible for us to live from them. The next few chapters will help you maintain and live out of a biblical view of yourself.

Father, thank you for choosing me when I did not choose you. Thank you for answering my very biggest needs of insecurity, fear, and shame and then making me a new creation in you. Thank you for adopting me into your family and making me new. Help me today to establish a view of myself that is consistent with how you view me—and then help me to learn to live from it. Amen.

7

PURSUE GOD: LIVING THE "WITH GOD" LIFE

Reunion with our Father is the primary work
that God is up to in your life and mine.[67]

— Morgan Snyder, *Becoming a King*

Whoever abides in me and I in him,
he it is that bears much fruit, for apart
from me you can do nothing.

— John 15:5, ESV

We were created to live the "with God" life—it's our divine purpose. The biblical account of creation tells us much about God's original design for us as his creation. Earlier (in Chapter 4) we talked about how God made us of his infinite matter. Now we'll dive again into these words that depict much more than just *how* God created us—it gives a picture of *who* God created us to be. It's easy to read the first two chapters of Genesis and see a list of events that show how God created us. But if we look a little closer, we'll see a clear picture of who God created us to be. Few verses stand out to me as profoundly as this passage from Colossians 1:15–17:

> [Jesus] is the image of the invisible God, the firstborn over all creation. For by him all things were created: things in heaven and on earth, visible and invisible, whether thrones or powers or rulers or authorities; all things were created by him and for him. He is before all things, and in him all things hold together.

Here we see how Paul views the creation account in Genesis. Jesus created us (and everything else): "For by him [Jesus] all things were created." That means God created us by his hand.

Paul also describes who Jesus is in the creation account: "He is before all things." These words don't just refer to the sequence of creation. Jesus is, along with the Father and the Holy Spirit, eternal. These words speak also of our place in creation; we exist beneath God. Not only did God create us by his hand, but also we exist in servitude under God's authority.

Finally, Paul tells what motivated God when he created us. These words should guide our day-to-day lives: "All things were created by him and for him." That last preposition matters! You and I exist *for* God.

In our world of self-centered importance, these words can be difficult to swallow. We live in a world that says we define our purpose. Nothing is more antithetical to the truth of God's Word, and nothing holds us back more from knowing God than believing we are the purpose for our lives. You and I were created in God's image, by God's hand, and for God's glory.

PLAY BALL!

We are a baseball family. Even my family members who don't really understand the game, its statistics, its strategies, or even its players are still fans of the game and of the St. Louis Cardinals. My grandfather routinely fell asleep in his chair watching Cardinals baseball. You could run through the room, jump up and down, and talk as loud as you wanted without waking him up. But if you were to walk over to the television, fade the volume down, and switch the channel, he'd immediately wake up.

You might not have a complete working knowledge of the game, but there's an illustration within the game that shows how to pursue the "with God" life. Major League Baseball (MLB) goes far beyond the teams that make up the American and National Leagues. Behind each MLB team like the St. Louis Cardinals is a "farm system" made up of minor league teams. As each minor league player develops skills, they move up the ranks of the farm system before graduating to fulfill their dream of playing Major League Baseball.

Think of walking with God in terms of an AAA (much like in baseball) approach. Understanding what the A's mean and working to apply them will help you walk closer with God. But only you can move up to the big leagues where you and God walk together daily. Focus on these three words:

- Authority
- Affinity
- Abiding

AUTHORITY

The entirety of the gospel can be summed up in just one word: kingdom. When you read the words of Jesus, you see he had one mission in mind: to bring the kingdom of God to earth. Consider these words of Jesus:

"The time promised by God has come at last!" he
announced. "The Kingdom of God is near! Repent of your
sins and believe the Good News!"[68]

The good news Jesus proclaimed was that the "Kingdom of God
is near." And it's not just that one passage! If you walk through
the Gospels and the book of Acts, you'll see time and again
where Jesus laid out his mission, what his disciples were to tell
people, and what the church was to proclaim: the kingdom of
God was near.[69]

So what is the Good News exactly? John Ortberg writes,
"Jesus' good news—his gospel—is simply this: the kingdom
of God has now, through Jesus, become available for ordinary
humans to live in."[70]

In Matthew 6 Jesus talked to people just like us—people
who got wrapped up in day-to-day lives. Like us, his listeners
were enamored with their clothes, their houses, and what they
ate and drank. People get distracted by these worries every day,
so Jesus was talking about them . . . and us too! Then he said
something you might have heard before:

But seek first the kingdom of God and his righteousness,
and all these things will be added to you.[71]

This begs a question, doesn't it? If Jesus came to deliver the kingdom of God, the disciples were sent to proclaim the kingdom of
God, the church was to further the kingdom of God, and we are
supposed to seek first the kingdom of God: What is the kingdom of God?

WHAT IS A KINGDOM?

Simply stated, a kingdom is "the range of one's effective will."[72] Look back at the first two chapters of Genesis. When God created everything, he did so within the range of his effective will—it was his kingdom.

The birds that flew in the air, the fish in the water, the mountains, the plants, the rivers—everything operated exactly as he designed and within his effective will. And for a time, even Adam and Eve acted under the effective will of God. God walked with Adam and Eve in the cool of the evening. They were obedient to God's instruction to enjoy all the garden but to steer clear of the Tree of Knowledge of Good and Evil. They operated under the authority of God's effective will and lived within the kingdom of God.

Did you know your will is a part of God's image in you? Think about it: God has a will he exercises over his kingdom, and so do you. Where did you get the drive to see your will done? You got it from God! But God desires you to *want* to exercise your will within his will.

What happened next has defined mankind since that day: Adam and Eve chose to section off God's kingdom into much smaller realms of *their own effective wills* . . . their own little kingdom. The same is true for us too. Now you see why it's so important for Jesus to bring the kingdom of heaven (God) to earth!

KINGDOMS BEGIN AND END WITH AUTHORITY

Kingdoms begin and end with authority, and God's kingdom is no exception. God intended us to live under his authority. If we intend to walk with God, we need to live under his authority. See again where Paul sets the limits of God's authority in our lives:

> He is before all things, and in him all things hold together.[73]

It's impossible for us to consider a relationship with God without understanding he comes before all things and is the glue that holds everything together. For us, that means God's intentions, values, and judgments are more valuable and truer than our own. If we are going to live the "with God" life, we need to surrender authority to him.

God intended us to live under his authority.

An interesting story about authority is in Matthew 8, where a centurion's servant was sick. This wasn't just any Roman guard. This guy was the real deal. He oversaw a lot of other soldiers. When he approached Jesus, he did something interesting because he understood authority. He asked Jesus to heal his servant, which Jesus agreed to do. But that's not the end of the story. The centurion said to Jesus:

> Lord, I am not worthy to have you come into my home. Just say the word from where you are, and my servant will be healed. I know this because I am under the authority of my superior officers, and I have authority over my soldiers. I only need to say "Go" and they go, or "Come" and they come. And if I say to my slaves, "Do this," they do it.[74]

The centurion understood authority because he commanded troops who did as instructed. He knew well that Jesus commanded authority over sickness—he'd heard of Jesus' miracles. If Jesus simply said the word, the sickness would leave because Jesus had authority over it. To develop a personal relationship with the Father, we must understand he is in authority over us, and we must choose to live under his authority.

HOW DOES AUTHORITY WORK IN REAL LIFE?

We all know when we start the car and release the brake that if we're not maintaining control of the wheel, it will move the direction it's pointed. Shortly after our oldest daughter, Marissa, learned to drive, she needed to pull the van into the garage. I wanted to close the garage door, so I instructed her to pull forward a little bit. She obediently released the brake and pressed the gas . . . and drove through the garage wall and into the dining room.

The same is true of God's authority in our lives. If we don't recognize God is in control and consciously surrender control to him, our lives will just move in the direction they're pointed. As Craig Groeschel said just as the world began to unravel in 2020, "God can do more through your surrender than you can with your control."[75]

AFFINITY

Authority alone can easily devolve into legalism. We don't mindlessly acknowledge God's authority. Even when we don't want to live under his authority, God graciously invites us not only to surrender to it but to love it. That's where affinity comes into play.

To have an affinity means to like or love something. It amazes me how often I love the things of this world and how easy it is not to value the things of God. For example:

I love to sleep. It's so much easier for me to sleep in an extra fifteen minutes and sacrifice spending time with God in the morning.

I love my stuff. It's so much easier for me to prioritize my possessions over seeing what God wants me to have or give away.

I love my opinions. It's so much easier for me to defend my political opinions vehemently than to align my views with God's views.

The difference between legalism and life-giving obedience to his authority is simply my love for it.

> LIVING THE "WITH GOD" LIFE REQUIRES ALLOWING
> MY RELATIONSHIP WITH GOD TO PERMEATE
> MY BODY AND MIND SO IT RESULTS IN AN
> AFFINITY FOR GOD'S WILL OVER MY OWN.

HOW DOES AFFINITY WORK IN REAL LIFE?

One influential writer in history was Nicholas Herman, a monk, who took the name Lawrence of the Resurrection. Brother Lawrence, as he came to be called, wanted so badly to develop an affinity for the presence of God that he intentionally chose to live in lowly conditions so he could find the presence of God in those circumstances. Time as a dishwasher and a repairman of sandals allowed Brother Lawrence to strip away the luxuries of life and still find joy in the presence of God. A series of letters was compiled after his death and is printed now as the seventeenth-century classic *The Practice of the Presence of God.*

One way to apply Lawrence's example is to list the least desirable parts of your life—the things you really don't enjoy doing. Maybe for you that's biding your time at work, mowing the lawn, or fixing the car. As you begin that activity, ask God to reveal his presence to you during that time and help you enjoy him there. It's a gutsy prayer! What if God shows up and reveals himself to you in those moments?

ABIDING

Abiding isn't a one-way street where you do all the work. In John 15, Jesus told us more about this two-way street:

> Abide in me, and I in you. As the branch cannot bear
> fruit by itself, unless it abides in the vine, neither can
> you, unless you abide in me. I am the vine; you are the
> branches. Whoever abides in me and I in him, he it is that
> bears much fruit, for apart from me you can do nothing.[76]

Don't read that too fast and miss it! When we abide in Jesus, he abides in us. That's big news! We aren't left to submit mindlessly to his authority and try our best to like it. Abiding in Jesus allows him to abide in us and develop the kind of character that will lead us to the rich and satisfying life that Jesus came to bring—the kind where his kingdom is available to us here and now!

HOW DOES ABIDING WORK IN REAL LIFE?

I am not a runner. If you see me running, I am probably being chased by an animal. The second I begin running for any reason I realize how short of breath I am. My breathing becomes very shallow as I grasp every single molecule of oxygen in complete desperation for life. But we can learn a great deal from avid runners, especially as it relates to breathing.

The act of breathing comes naturally. We don't have to think about it; it just happens. But if our bodies exert effort, they have a greater need for oxygen. People like me resort to short, shallow breaths. But the best runners retrain their breathing rhythms.

My sister-in-law Stephanie is one of those avid runners. She's run the Chicago Marathon several times and is training to qualify for Boston. She taught me different runners try different methods of regulating their breathing. Some runners don't really have to try techniques for regulating their breathing, and other runners need to be far more intentional.

Deep, slow, rhythmic breaths allow your lungs to fill with oxygen. This intentional act of filling your lungs with oxygen gives your body time to process the fuel before you expel it and start over. Abiding in Christ is just like that. Dallas Willard taught that abiding in Christ is breathing in deeply the words of Christ and allowing them to respirate our hearts.[77] We can't expect our hearts to be filled with short, shallow breaths of Jesus.

ABIDING IN JESUS ISN'T ABOUT JUST STAYING STRONG BUT ESTABLISHING A RHYTHM OF RESPIRATION FOR OUR SOULS.

These words of Jesus are crucial for us: "Apart from me you can do nothing." Just as we can't take another step without breathing, we can't live the "with God" life without abiding in Christ. Know this for sure: we can realize God is in authority, but we'll never be able to develop an affinity for him without abiding in him.

Remember, living the "with God" life isn't about mindless obedience or a life of religious obligation. The "with God" life finds him in a place of authority over you, where you develop a deep affinity for him and allow your heart to abide in him. A phrase resounds with me right now as I consider this idea: "I can't do this without you." For just a moment, consider the deeper meaning of that phrase. On the surface, it means I've got most of what it takes to overcome this circumstance, but without God's final *umph* to get me over the finish line, I won't make it. But there's much more to it. Maybe I should rephrase it: "I can't do this apart from you!"

God, I can't do this life apart from you. You are the life-giving source. You hold me together and give me purpose to live. Not only do I need the umph *you give to get me over the finish line, but I also need your sustaining power in my everyday life. Will you help me lean away from empty religion and toward the journey you're calling me to take with you? Amen.*

8

PURSUE TRUTH: LIVING THROUGH THE LENS OF TRUTH

Make [Christianity] attractive, make good men
wish it were true, and then show them that it is.

— Blaise Pascal

I don't know if you've noticed or not, but the world is falling apart like a leper on a treadmill. In 2020 alone, we weathered a worldwide pandemic, we navigated a ridiculously turbulent (and polarizing) presidential campaign, riots broke out in the streets, two hurricanes struck the Gulf of Mexico at the same time, people cried out to defund the very organizations that keep them safe, church attendance was down by at least 50 percent or more across the country—all while we teetered on complete financial collapse around the globe. I wanted to call my mom and ask if her offer to slap me into next year still stood.

Never in the history of mankind has it been more crucial to view the world through a biblical lens. That is the heartbeat behind the idea of Pursue Truth: to pursue a biblical perspective of the world. My hope isn't to cover this topic exhaustively but to introduce an idea that should take us on a lifetime journey toward Jesus and seeing the world through his eyes.

Doing so will allow us to see what's happening around us differently and lead us to ask much deeper, more revealing questions. For instance, when we encounter a turbulent election, we'll be challenged to loosen our political opinions to understand God's will for our political system and how he wants us to participate. When we face economic collapse, our hearts' deep desires for security will be exposed. When we see people treated unjustly because of the color of their skin, we'll argue less about what we think is right and wrong and develop a biblical perspective on their plight through God's eyes. It's not *as important* where we land on these issues as it is that we come to those conclusions through our journey with Jesus.

OUR INFALLIBLE RESOURCE

Believe it or not, a time existed when you could generally depend on the news you saw or read. That's hard to believe in a world with the popular phrase "fake news." Today, the news is inundated with sources claiming to be completely true that, upon investigation, are extremely biased. This doesn't just apply to political opinions but to every possible perspective. This crazy phenomenon leads me to ask whom I can trust and where absolute truth can be found.

In the world of social media, I see more and more conversations about "fact finding." Take, for instance, the issue of treatment for COVID-19. If you scrolled through Facebook in 2020, you probably found references to the drug hydroxychloroquine. (I'm a pastor. I don't have a useful opinion on this issue. If you want to know what Ephesians 5 is about, I'm your man. When it comes to medicine, you should ask a medical expert!) But when you read about the drug, undoubtedly Facebook alerted you that the World Health Organization didn't authorize it as treatment for COVID-19. What were we supposed to believe? I later had a conversation with a doctor and asked him about the treatment. What he said was alarming. He believed the news sources were so politically motivated and filtered that we couldn't even depend on the information being posited in pursuit of a treatment for a worldwide pandemic!

The issue of infallible truth is even more pressing when I step beyond politics or social issues and delve into how I should view the world around me.

> **WE ALL LINE UP AT A BUFFET OF INFORMATION SORTING THROUGH OPTIONS FOR SOMETHING THAT IS TRUE AND DEPENDABLE, YET WE'RE UNSURE IF WHAT WE'LL CONSUME WILL HELP US OR POTENTIALLY KILL US.**

As a follower of Christ, I'm thankful we have one resource we don't need to question, and it still stands up to all our questions: the Bible. In developing a view of the world through the lens of the Bible, we must believe God's Word is not only objective but also objectively true. If we struggle to accept the wisdom of Scripture at face value as objectively authoritative in our lives, we'll continue to depend on the obviously biased and fallible resources of the world.

The Bible is God's divinely inspired Word. Look at what Paul writes to Timothy:

> All Scripture is breathed out by God and profitable for teaching, for reproof, for correction, and for training in

righteousness, that the man of God may be complete, equipped for every good work.[78]

Paul's words are crucial to our developing worldview. When he says, "All Scripture is breathed out by God," we need to take note. We're going to dip our toes into some deep waters for a minute. Don't stop reading; we won't be here long.

Our view of Scripture isn't just that God "inspired" it so we should see some similarities between what we read and what God intended. In the early '90s, the rapper Vanilla Ice had a famous song: "Ice Ice Baby." Remember the bassline hook at the beginning? *Dun dun du du dun.* At the time, if you were a fan of more classic rock like Queen, you immediately recognized the riff from the song "Under Pressure." Despite the groundbreaking litigation that resulted in what we now know as "sampling," we see this typical definition of the word "inspiration"—a song or work that influences another song. That's not the same inspiration as when we talk about the Bible.

The Greek word Paul uses for what we translate as "breathed out by God" is the compound Greek word *theopneustos.* Paul's not saying God inspired Scripture like Queen inspired Vanilla Ice. Rather, God breathed the words of Scripture directly into the minds and the pens (okay, quills) of the original authors of the original biblical manuscripts. For us, that means the words of Scripture are literally and specifically inspired *directly* by God's Holy Spirit.

One more wiggle of our toes in these deep waters and we'll get back to where we live: as believers in this divinely inspired Word of God, we believe in verbal plenary inspiration of Scripture. This means God used different men with different writing styles to write exactly what he wanted to be written in the Scriptures. Every single word came directly from God. The Bible as we hold it today is God's Word to us. It "reliably fixes the boundaries of everything he will ever say to humankind."[79] To us, that essentially means everything God says through his Word is true, but it does not mean everything that is true is contained in his Word.

> The Bible "reliably fixes the boundaries of everything [God] will ever say to humankind."
> — Dallas Willard

To say something is true because it claims to be true is a logical fallacy known as "circular reasoning." I don't accept the Bible is true because it claims to be true. I accept the Bible claims to be true because it is true.

If you can't accept the Bible is true and has authority over your life, then it will be necessary to part ways here, at least for the time being. There is no substitute for the diligent study of Scripture in the life of a Christ follower.

OUR VALUABLE YET FALLIBLE RESOURCE

Relationships demand communication. Healthy relationships demand ongoing, healthy communication. Remember, God's primary work in your life is developing your reunion with him.[80] That kind of relationship takes ongoing conversation and interaction. The Bible firmly lays the foundation and "reliably fixes the boundaries"[81] for that relationship. But God's communication with his children continues today.[82]

Let me illustrate it this way. A man and his wife are in the office of a marriage counselor. After several meetings together, the wife finally expresses what's bothering her: "He hasn't told me that he loves me since our wedding day."

Defeated, the husband offers his only justification. "Baby, I told you that I loved you when we got married. I just figured if that changed, I'd let you know."

That's no way to communicate with someone you love deeply. Our relationship with God is no different.

Throughout the Scriptures, we see God speaking audibly to his people: Adam and Eve, Noah, Abraham, Jacob, Moses, to the apostle Paul at his conversion, and countless other examples. Are these examples of how God spoke to his people? Or were they *exceptions* only for special people at special moments?

In John 10, Jesus explained:

> The gatekeeper opens the gate for him, and the sheep recognize his voice and come to him. He calls his own sheep by name and leads them out.[83]

Jesus' sheep know his voice because they're familiar with the sound of his voice. You must listen closely for the voice of your loving shepherd who calls you. God's voice is available if you'll stop, listen for it, and move forward when you hear it.

But God is not like the husband in our example of the marriage counseling office. He never changes. When we follow God's voice, he will never lead us in contradiction to his Word. God's written Word is infallible. Yet our understanding of what God leads us to do is anything but infallible.

There isn't enough room here to dive too deeply into how this works in day-to-day life. But we can establish the foundation for this conversational intimacy, and then take the first steps of learning to listen. The study beyond this is vast and seemingly never-ending. I listed a few resources that will help you wade into these deep waters.[84]

For now, let's learn the basics of listening to God's voice in real life.[85]

START SIMPLE

Don't start trying to listen to God's voice on a big decision such as moving away or getting married. Try to listen for God's leading when less is at stake. For instance, maybe begin by asking God if you should have a friend over for dinner.

TEST IT OUT

Once you ask the question, start trying on the options. *God, are you saying you want me to have the Smiths over for dinner? Or are you saying I shouldn't have the Smiths over for dinner?* You'll quickly see how trying on the options will allow you to listen closely for God's lead. I know it seems ridiculous to put so much effort into a decision to have a friend over for dinner, but this isn't about dinner. It's about creating a safe place to hear God's voice so you can know what it sounds like when making bigger decisions.

TRY IT OUT

Now that you tried the options on to sense God's leading, it's time to try it out. Pick an option that you feel like God is leading you toward and see how it goes. Once it's over, revisit with God and talk with him about how it went and how you can be more sensitive to hearing his voice.

Remember, the goal here isn't to choose every action correctly—it's not a batting average. The goal is to walk in unison with your Father within the boundaries of his written Word. The goal is conversational intimacy with God.

WHAT'S THE RESULT?

The world can look so small when you're stuck in the day-to-day grind. Imagine if you took this book and pressed it directly against the skin of your nose. You wouldn't be able to see much more than a few letters or a word or two. But when you hold it at a distance, you can see much more.

Our family went on vacation several years ago to East Tennessee to stay in the Great Smoky Mountains. It's beautiful to drive through and look at the trees and see a winding creek dancing in and out of the woods alongside the road. But I was blown away when we hiked to the top of Clingmans Dome—the highest point in the range. From just over 6,600 feet above sea level on a clear day, you can see for more than 100 miles in each direction. It's a breathtaking view! Each step you climb up the half-mile road to the dome changes the way you see the trees around you. Why? Because your perspective changes your perception. In like manner, as you grow in developing a biblical view of the world, your perception of the world changes.

SEE PEOPLE THROUGH GOD'S EYES

Parents are notorious for their proverbial wisdom embodied in little sayings. Sayings such as "People who live in glass houses shouldn't throw stones" or "Sticks and stones may break my bones, but words will never hurt me" are just a couple of them. They may or may not always be true, but they're nevertheless the soundtrack for many children's upbringings. One more that comes to mind is "You can't judge a book by its cover."

The problem is our human perspectives often judge books by their covers. We can't see inside a person any more than we can see past a book's cover. To get a deeper look into a book, we must open it up and read. When it comes to people, it's even more difficult. But when we develop a biblical view of the world, we see people around us with a bit more of what God sees when he sees them . . . and us. Perspective changes perception.

When we encounter a difficult person, the most challenging issue isn't how to deal with them—it's how to develop compassion for them. When we naturally make a judgment based on how someone looks or by the color of their skin, the biggest problem isn't realizing what we've done but understanding why we did it and what's true about them. When we meet someone lost in addiction, understanding what they were searching for is what allows us to move beyond judgment and help them. Perspective changes perception.

SEE TIME THROUGH GOD'S EYES

When we view the world through God's eyes, we see events that have happened differently. It also dramatically changes how we see what's going to happen—and our roles in the future.

The cross is no longer just a historical event. The cross also is, for us, many things—too many to dive into here. Not only is it the conduit through which God offers salvation, but the cross also is the succinct picture of God demonstrating his rule over sin.

Sin never had power that God didn't allow it to have. Sin is our effort to create lives other than what God intended for us.

The cross is the perfect picture of God demonstrating his sovereignty over the sin of our independence.

As we hone our biblical view of the world, God shows how he has already demonstrated his power over sin. He also extends the invitation to join at his side ruling over sin day to day. As we grow in our relationship with him, we gradually settle into our roles in this world of training to become kings who will rule and reign with the King of kings!

SEE YOUR ROLE THROUGH GOD'S EYES

When we view the world through a biblical lens, we quickly realize we live in a world at war. I'm not talking about the wars we hear about in the news where one people group is against another over a piece of land or a political ideal. The world we live in is at war on a spiritual plane.

The kingdom of God is in constant war with the kingdom of darkness. God calls us to be warriors in those daily battles. The question isn't if we're at war; rather, the question is if we'll engage.

At the end of Ephesians, Paul writes some sobering words to the church:

> A final word: Be strong in the Lord and in his mighty power. Put on all of God's armor so that you will be able to stand firm against all strategies of the devil. For we are not fighting against flesh-and-blood enemies, but against evil rulers and authorities of the unseen world, against mighty powers in this dark world, and against evil spirits in the heavenly places.[86]

The "strategies of the devil" are unavoidable. That's how opposition works. If we could avoid them, they wouldn't be opposition.

> The "strategies of the devil" are unavoidable.

But Paul poses two weapons that are available to us: strength and armor. The strength isn't just our own intestinal fortitude—that's courage. Paul talks about a supernatural strength that comes to us through our relationship with the King of kings who has sovereign power over the kingdom of darkness. The extent to which we see the world around us biblically is the extent to which we'll be able to suit up in our armor and fight well. In the succeeding verses in Ephesians, Paul gives us pieces of the Christian's armor:

> Therefore, put on every piece of God's armor so you will be able to resist the enemy in the time of evil. Then after the battle you will still be standing firm. Stand your ground, putting on the belt of truth and the body armor of God's righteousness. For shoes, put on the peace that comes from the Good News so that you will be fully prepared. In addition to all of these, hold up the shield of faith to stop the fiery arrows of the devil. Put on salvation as your helmet, and take the sword of the Spirit, which is the word of God. Pray in the Spirit at all times and on every occasion. Stay alert and be persistent in your prayers for all believers everywhere.[87]

Followers of Christ are called into battle. Outfitted with these critical armaments, we stand strong against the efforts of the devil. Only in the "with God" life, guided by his view of the world, will we find any dependable footing against the enemy.

129

Following Jesus without a dependable resource that we can stand on is impossible. God gives us everything we need in his eternal Word. Without it, we exist on shaky ground. As we grow in our knowledge of his Word, we're increasingly able to see the world around us through the lens of what is real and dependable. Without his Word, we're left to the changing winds of culture. As we lean into his Word, we can hear his voice. Without it, we can only discern his leading based on our fallible emotions. He has sovereignly given us every vital resource we need to build the foundation of our faith and engage in the battles that we fight against our enemy every day.

Jesus, I confess that my own perspective, values, and emotions tend to rule my world. I realize you have given me everything I need to build the foundation of my faith in your eternal Word. I want to shift my allegiances from leaning on my own understanding to leaning on your Word. Please help me to increasingly value the dependability of your Word. Amen.

9

PURSUE AUTHENTICITY: LIVING THE HEALED LIFE

We live amid a terrible tragedy, one of our own making. Our lives lack the focus and synergy God created them to have. We lead terribly disintegrated lives. As a result, we compartmentalize our work lives from our home lives, our relationships from our struggles, and worst yet, the entirety of our lives from our relationship with God. This disintegration is at the heart of our struggle and why we fall into the "believe and behave" faith that leaves us so empty. We have somehow found a way to separate our relationship with God from our worship of him. God wants us to live in complete, integrated fellowship with him as our creator and sustainer, but we can't live in integrated fellowship with God until we are confident in who we are as individuals.

God didn't intend for life to be so fractionalized. This fraction is why we struggle to find redeeming value in our religious efforts—they just don't connect across the barriers we've constructed to separate the parts of our life from the whole. As a result, the core of who we are is disconnected from the parts. It's much like those gears we discussed. We can't expect the parts of our lives to function well without meshing the gears together as they were designed.

WE BARELY UNDERSTAND INTEGRATION ANYMORE

When we use the word "integration," one enduring example resounds in my ears. Maybe the antonym for "integration" will bring that example to your mind: segregation.

Prior to the efforts of heroes of the civil rights movement, such as Dr. Martin Luther King, Jr., schools across the country were separated by color. Black and white children were separated not only by their neighborhoods but by the color of their skin.

Many white people didn't even realize there was a problem. After all, they were safe and cared for in their well-funded safe havens. Black children and their families, on the other hand, knew all too well of the disparity between their educational system and the one offered to their white counterparts.

Amid those insanely turbulent times, schools became integrated—black children were bussed to formerly all-white schools. That should have solved the problem, right? I think not. While the racial integration of schools was a much better solution than segregating them, what we accomplished fell massively short of guaranteeing basic human rights to an otherwise completely disenfranchised people. Essentially, we took black children from their neighborhoods, cultures, and family structures and then plopped them into a foreign land. We didn't integrate them; we desegregated them.

Not enough words can be written to address the ramifications of all that happened to bring basic human dignity to people of color. But this is a great example of our complete misunderstanding of integration. Simply desegregating something is a far cry from the hard work of integrating.

JESUS IS OUR MODEL

Early elementary children sit in a semi-circle in a typical Sunday school room. The smell of crayons and construction paper fills the air, and each child wears their "Sunday best" as the octogenarian teacher enters the room carrying what seems to be a box covered with a flowing, black cloth.

She addresses the children: "Class, underneath this cloth I have a surprise! Let's see if you can guess what it is!" The class listens with interest as the teacher describes in detail the contents of the package. "It's yellow. It has wings. And it sits on a perch. Does anyone have a guess?"

Without hesitation, one child pipes up, "Teacher, I'm not sure what's under there. It sure sounds like a canary, but since we're in Sunday school, I'm going to guess it's Jesus!"

I know that's an old joke (at least it is to me), but it serves us well to understand what we're talking about. In church circles, we learn from a young age that "Jesus is the answer." But doesn't it depend on the question?

The question is: What does a fully integrated life with the Father resemble? To that question, Jesus *is* the answer. As Morgan Snyder said, "Jesus' life had a quality of eternity as he rested in the strength of his Father."[88] In every moment we observe Jesus in the Scriptures, he lived fully and completely integrated with the Father. Jesus modeled the perfect connection with the Father.

Jesus is a perfect picture of perfection. In him we see not only a picture of perfect connection with the Father but also a picture of someone in perfect sync with himself. We have a better chance of seeing a unicorn than we do a person today who walks in sync with their true self. To find a safe place, we often hide behind something.

For instance, the root word behind the word "personality" is the Latin word *persona*, which was commonly used by actors in the ancient theater to describe the masks behind which they hid.

THUS, YOUR PERSONALITY MAY BE A MASK THAT YOU HIDE BEHIND TO FIND A SAFE PLACE TO EXPRESS YOURSELF.

That's what happens when we live disintegrated lives. We're forced to find safe ways to express ourselves, safe places to ask the questions that burn in our hearts: *Am I _____ (strong, beautiful, smart, etc.) enough? Do I have what it takes? Am I safe?*

This might sound like some kind of self-help talk, but consider that the self-help movement is a godless effort to counterfeit the healing work of God to help us live fully integrated lives. No matter how long we stare into a mirror and repeat the immortal words of the *Saturday Night Live* character Stuart Smalley, "I'm good enough. I'm smart enough, and doggone it, people like me,"[89] the words will never have enough power to overshadow the deeply embedded words of our enemy that tell us otherwise.

That's right. Our common enemy is in the business of tearing down who we are and how we see ourselves. But tearing down how we see ourselves is not enough for him. The enemy also wants to tear down how we think God sees us.

UNDERSTANDING THE TRUE YOU

Before we understand the truth about who we are, we need to address the truth about who we *are not.* We've all heard the word "sinner" used to describe ourselves. Romans 3:23 says, "For everyone has sinned; we all fall short of God's glorious standard." Dozens of scriptures refer to our sins, as a matter of fact. But you'll never find a follower of Jesus described by his former, sin-stained state. For instance, Jesus described the Pharisees as white-washed tombs, made to look great on the outside, but rotting to death on the inside. But Jesus never referred to his followers by who they were before they followed him. In other words: to Jesus, you are not your sin nature—you are not who you used to be. As a follower of Christ, your "old life is gone; a new life has begun!" (2 Cor. 5:17).

Another verse people quote to associate our brokenness in our day-to-day life is Jeremiah 17:9:

The heart is deceitful above all things
and beyond cure. Who can understand it?[90]

Your heart is made desperately wicked by sin's controlling of it. We all have sinned, and we fall short of God's glory on our own. That doesn't sound like great news, does it? But understand one vital truth: you are not your sin nature.

Sin is what you do to find a life that's worth living apart from Jesus. Sin isn't just the desperate act of the addict scratching around in an alley trying to find a used needle. We can all see the sin in that. Whether it's addiction to a chemical, an inner striving to make a little more money,

> Sin is living apart from Jesus

or the nagging need to be a person of influence—all these sins are examples of our sin nature speaking much louder than our true nature as blood-bought, adopted sons and daughters of the King, who are invited to grow into our future roles reigning alongside the King. Those lesser temptations only offer a counterfeit version of the rich and satisfying life Jesus offers.

John Eldredge says, "The real you is on the side of God against the false self."[91] At this point, you may be asleep on the front lines while the battle for your heart rages around you. But there is a battle for your heart, you are on God's side, and if you'll pursue the true you, there is a far "[richer] and satisfying life" than you can imagine!

WHAT KEEPS YOU FROM LIVING AS THE TRUE YOU?

Like we talked about in Chapter 7, filtering everything through the biblical worldview that's available to us through Scripture is important. Follow this thought with me.

- Satan is our enemy.
- Our enemy is a liar.
- Our enemy's agenda is to steal, kill, and destroy.
- Our enemy cannot take you from God's hand, but he can deceive you into *passive acquiescence* rather than *active opposition* to him.[92]

I won't even pretend that what I'll write here will even begin to answer all the pressing, deep questions of pain your heart is asking right now. But I can introduce you to *a part of the way* that I see our enemy is at work in our everyday lives and how God brings healing. Much has been written to help you along this journey. You can delve deeper into these ideas by reading some of the resources and conversations I listed in the endnotes.[93]

EVERY PAIN LEAVES A WOUND

Like most kids, I fell. Unlike most kids, I fell down a lot! I've never been very coordinated. I remember getting off the bus at maybe seven years old. When I stepped off the last step, I somehow tripped and fell. As I hit the pavement, I did more than scratch up my knee. I cut it—a lot. I might be a bit dramatic here, but blood was everywhere. Once my mom picked me up and I stopped sobbing, we had the hard work of picking the tiny bits of gravel out of my knee. I still have the scar to remember the moment.

God's design of our bodies is not much different than his design of our hearts. When our body has an open wound, foreign matter (in my case, gravel) can get into the wound, which leads to infection. Our hearts aren't much different.

When we go through painful moments in our lives, inevitably there's an open wound. Disappointment as a child, harsh words lashed out in anger, betrayals, and bullying are just a few examples of the deeply wounding moments we all experience.

Those wounds are a perfect place for foreign objects to become lodged. But they're not as obvious as gravel. The lies we hear from the enemy get lodged in our open, wounded hearts and will fester for years to come. If we don't clear them out, our hearts become infected by the lies we hear.

EVERY WOUND LEAVES A MESSAGE

Opportunity is what the enemy looks for. The last few words of Jesus' encounter with Satan in Luke 4 are interesting to me:

> When the devil had finished all this tempting, he left him until an opportune time.[94]

The enemy looks for opportunities to grab ahold of your heart. Every time you experience pain, the enemy waits in the wings to whisper something to you, hoping that amidst the pain of the moment you won't notice. In my experience, the enemy gives his tainted take on how this painful moment came to be, his perspective as to how it's your fault, or his explanation of how you could have avoided it altogether.

Remember, the enemy isn't all that creative. He's just consistent. He's pulled this junk in people's lives for millennia. What happens next is the critical component. Being told a lie is one thing, but believing it is another.

EVERY MESSAGE OFFERS AN AGREEMENT

Our wounded moments leave us very susceptible to suggestion. Those moments in addition to our sin nature and our disintegrated relationship with God leave us particularly susceptible to messages that come from the enemy. What the enemy looks for is simple: he wants us to agree with his tainted perspective on who we are.

I'll share a personal story with you. It's painful to me, but I hope the risk of telling something like this will help you see what I'm talking about.

I was bullied a lot in my early teen years. Unfortunately, that's not at all unusual. What might have been unusual was the amount and severity of those interactions. All those fights came with undeniable messages from the enemy through the voices of those aggressors.

One of the primary people who consistently picked on me culminated their efforts one day in front of approximately twenty of my peers. He approached me, pretending to talk to me as if he were going to be kind, while another friend of his ducked down behind me. Once his friend was in position, the bully shoved me over him, and they both jumped on me and severely beat me up. He then climbed on top of me and said, "You're such a —." His insult had to do with my being weak.

Completely demoralized and ashamed, I struggled to gather my books, and I ran to the first safe place I could find while they all laughed. While I was in the bathroom trying to get the blood off my face and clothes, I kept repeating the bully's words in the mirror through the tears.

What happened there was much more significant than some bruises, cuts, and a bloody nose—those things heal on their own with time. And it wasn't just my pride that was damaged that day. That too healed with time. But the message the enemy voiced through the bully's mouth took decades to heal.

A message accompanied the wounds that day and left me with two options: agreement or defense. Had I not been so damaged by countless instances like that one, I might have been able to see it hadn't been a fair fight. But weakened by too many of these, I had no defense, and I agreed with the message of the enemy.

AGREEMENTS BECOME OUR STARTING POINTS

More than thirty years later, I can stand in a group of men today and feel like the weakest one in the group regardless of my size or strength in comparison. What's worse is that it's not only a feeling. Unchecked today, this decades-old agreement that I'm weak becomes a starting point for me. Something I feel like I must prove it's not true.

So as a result of this incident, I tend to resort to different efforts to prove my strength (mainly to myself): grandiose storytelling, arrogance, not allowing others to have the last word, or using degrading words to others, just to name a few.

Living under agreements with the enemy is not the rich and satisfying life Jesus wants for me. When I read where Jesus said he came to heal the brokenhearted and set the captives free, I know he wants me to find freedom from the agreements I've made with the enemy.

So where does healing come from? I didn't get to this place overnight. The enemy has worked to refortify those agreements dozens—maybe hundreds—of times since then. There's more to healing than just figuring out what's not true. You've not just heard these lies; you've wholeheartedly believed them. If you want freedom from them, you must tear them out at the root!

BREAKING AGREEMENTS LEADS TO FREEDOM

The freedom God offers is not found simply in the information we believe; it's found in relationship with Jesus. The Spirit-led work of identifying those agreements, digging them up by the roots, and replacing them with the truth of God's

> Freedom is found in relationship with Jesus.

Word leads to freedom. Living in that freedom leads to the healing God wants to bring. To make sure this stays well above the "self-help" counterfeit, it's important to note a few crucial pieces of that puzzle.

First, identifying those agreements isn't just about listing the most painful moments in your life; it begins with God leading us to those moments. The freedom God wants for you is as much in the relationship with him as it is in the circumstances of the agreement. Uprooting those lies isn't as simple as saying, *I'm not* _____ (fill in the blank with your own reality) and replacing the information. If you're going to find divine freedom, the Holy Spirit needs to lead you in identifying the lies and agreements. Often, you can't really understand beyond the surface level of your agreements without God's intimate understanding of your heart.

Second, the truth we place into the gaping hole when we uproot those lies needs to be more valuable than what we've removed. We can't simply take those out and replace them with the opposite—we need to understand what God said in his Word and replace the lies with that truth.

LIVING IN FREEDOM LEADS TO HEALING

The healing of those wounds and agreements doesn't come from just finding the lies and replacing them. True healing comes as I walk day after day, renewing my commitment to what is true about me, and speaking through the power of the Holy Spirit to the enemy with reminders that his words have no power over me.

This is true in other areas of life as well. You don't become a great runner by knowing about running or a great chef by knowing about cooking. You become great by doing those activities over time. Malcolm Gladwell noted in his book *Outliers* that for a person to become an expert in any area of expertise, they need to log a minimum of ten thousand hours in practice.[95] Freedom from the messages of the enemy comes immediately when we, walking and speaking in the Spirit, claim the power of the resurrected Christ over the message of the enemy. Healing comes from walking in that freedom! If you had been locked in prison for years and were suddenly eligible for release, the decision of the court to release you doesn't mean anything until you take the steps out of your cell. *Living* in freedom is what releases you from the prison of your agreements, not just *acknowledging* your freedom.

> Healing comes from walking day after day in freedom.

If people knew that the true offer of the gospel was healing from the things that hold our hearts back, they would be tearing the roofs off churches to get inside.

TRY IT OUT!

This isn't a theory: it's *real* and *practical*. You can try this out right now. Begin this journey with Jesus today. Ask him to lead your mind to a particular wounding moment in your story. It might be a story like mine where you were wounded at the hand of another, or your story might involve a particularly traumatizing moment when you lost a loved one. Understanding everything about the moment is not as important as being able to articulate the message and the accompanying agreement. This isn't just walking through your story but walking through your story *with Jesus*.

Now ask God to help you identify the lie the enemy told you, and then ask God to help you understand what is true about you from his eyes. Finally, speak God's truth over the lie and break that agreement. Begin to walk in that freedom, and healing will come as your relationship with Jesus allows space for the healing to begin.

You can't separate the work that God wants to do in your life tomorrow from the pain you experienced yesterday, much less the lies you believed along the way. When you believe lies, it's far more catastrophic than just what you believe to be true— you live *from* those lies. If you're going to find victory, you need to live as the "true you" that you were created to be, not the false self you've constructed from your pain. Freedom in Christ isn't a vague concept; it's victory over the darkness that you've inadvertently let into your daily life.

Jesus, my life has been riddled with pain, disappointment, unmet expectations, and betrayal. I'm thankful that you want more for me than just overlooking my pain. I'm thankful that you want to walk with me through my pain and heal those broken places in my heart and root out the lies that I believe about myself and the world around me. Help me see where you're offering your healing work in my story next. Amen.

10

PURSUE RELATIONSHIPS: LIVING WITH LIKE-MINDED PEOPLE

Louis Zamperini was by all measures an incredible man. A WWII veteran, an Olympic runner, and later in life, because of the transformative power of God, a Christian evangelist. Raised in a poor Italian family, Louis realized in high school that he had an amazing ability to run . . . fast! Fueled by the encouragement of his brother, he continued to train until he competed at the Olympic level. While he placed eighth in the 1936 Olympics, he set a record for the fastest lap to date.

But that's not the most amazing feat of his life. Louis survived being stranded on a lifeboat longer than anyone else in history. His bomber plane experienced mechanical problems and crashed into the Pacific Ocean, killing eight of the eleven men on board, and leaving Louis to float aimlessly for forty-seven days. After this, the Japanese captured him as a prisoner of war. Louis knew well what it meant to be alone.

Have you seen the History Channel's *Alone?* On the show, ten men, equipped with only ten items of their choosing, are dropped into isolation in a part of the world. Each man battles to find shelter and food and safety from wildlife, armed only with their wits, experience, and the ten items they chose. But the most challenging obstacle is isolation. Some brave the harsh elements unbelievably well only to succumb to the haunting reality of seclusion. All these stories have one thing in common: survival. None of them thrives in isolation; they all merely figure out a way to survive.

We are a people created for relationship. We each need it differently, but we each need it equally. Someone might find the idea of being isolated for some amount of time attractive or even comforting, but we weren't intended to live in isolation from people.

WE THINK WE CAN DO THIS ALONE

I've been ministering in the local church for almost three decades now. I'm often tempted to think ministry would be easier if it weren't for people. People and relationships are among the most rewarding—and challenging—aspects of ministry.

People are messy, fickle, and inconsistent (just to name a few). Even as I write this, I'm reminded of times where each of those qualities is also true of myself. Couple that with the reality that as we live with people, sharing our victories, challenges, and insecurities, we leave ourselves open to betrayal and disappointment. We can easily think life is safer without people—or at least we should be very guarded about the people we allow close to us. And to be completely fair, it is safer. It's by no means better, but it is safer.

When God created relationships between people, he did so first with Adam and Eve. But recall first in Genesis 1 how after every day of creation God noted each object created was good. Then, he created Adam to rule over it all. But in Genesis 2, he said something entirely different:

The LORD God said, "It is *not good* for the man to be alone. I will make a helper suitable for him."[96]

Get that? Everything God created was good as it stood: alone. But it was *not good* for man to be alone. Adam did not have everything he needed to succeed by himself, so God created a helper for him. Now, in this context, God refers to creating Eve, Adam's "helper alongside."[97]

Would it have been easier for Adam to rule over God's creation alone? If you've been married for more than ten minutes, you'll probably agree it might have been easier but not better.

> **WHEN WE LIVE WITH THOSE WHOM GOD CREATED TO BE "HELPERS ALONGSIDE," LIFE IS NOT ALWAYS EASIER, BUT IT'S BETTER.**

YOU'RE BETTER WHEN IT'S BETTER

Acts tells of the beginning of the church. But Acts is not just the history *of* the church, it's the vision God intended *for* the church. If multiple people are involved in a project, it can often gravitate toward complexity and away from its original purpose. The same is true of biblical community. Look at how the church started:

They devoted themselves to the apostles' teaching and to the fellowship, to the breaking of bread and to prayer. Everyone was filled with awe, and many wonders and miraculous signs were done by the apostles. All the believers were together and had everything in common. . . . Every day they continued to meet together in the temple courts. They broke bread in their homes and ate together with glad and sincere hearts.[98]

Look at the words Luke used to describe the church: *devoted, filled with awe, glad,* and *sincere.* Are those words you would use to describe your most recent meetings with other Christians? Probably not.

But what happened to being devoted and filled with awe? Being glad? Being sincere? Is it the fault of the church, or do we not benefit from community because we don't invest in it? For a follower of Christ, community is like the stock market: we can't cash a check from it until we've invested in it.

THE REALITY OF LIMITED RESOURCES

I get it. I feel the same way! There are too many things to do around the house, games to get to, work piles up at the office, and the schedule never seems to cooperate. Then there's the internal pull. *What if someone asks me something, and I don't know the answer?* I'd feel exposed. *What if I invest, and I'm the only one?* I'd feel like I wasted my time. You know the excuses as well as I do.

The bottom line is, as Morgan Snyder says, "Peer relationships are intended to be oxygen for our . . . soul."[99] If we want to live like God intended us to live, we can't thrive without people alongside us, journeying with us. If we're going to live fueled by excuses, we'll live inevitably limited by them.

WHAT'S THE SOLUTION?

The solution? Invest. But the trick isn't holding up a sign for people to join you or joining a community group at church in hopes you'll find the right people. You start by becoming the *kind of person* Christians want to be around. You might find those people in a community group, but you won't find them until you become a person with whom people want to join forces.

The movie *Gladiator* takes place circa AD 180 at the height of the Roman Empire. The main character, Maximus, and a band of fellow prisoners are on the floor of the Colosseum facing what is almost undoubtedly the end of their lives. Maximus, the self-appointed leader of this band of undernourished prisoners, gathers his men closely and says the words we would all love to hear when facing uncertain times: "Whatever comes out of these gates, we have a better chance of survival if we work together."[100]

Who wouldn't want to fight alongside warriors who have your best interest and victory in the battle as their highest values? But you can't just sign up for that relationship; it's a relationship that's developed. These are the kinds of people with whom we need to partner.

> You have to develop a relationship.

BECOMING THE RIGHT KIND OF PERSON

Talk about a nebulous idea. The idea of becoming the kind of person with whom people will want to partner on life's journey toward Jesus is vague. But we can all agree something significant is here. We all need partners, in good times and in bad. If people trust us and want to help shoulder our burdens, we could be well on our way to the devotion, awe, gladness, and sincerity the first-century believers experienced in their community.

The first step is carrying your own burdens with sincerity and diligence. Let's face it, nobody wants to take your burdens more seriously than you do. Conversely, when others sincerely want more out of their faith journey, there isn't much you won't do to help them. Expecting people to treat your struggles and obstacles with sincerity if you won't do the same is impossible. But if you've read this far in the book, you're on your way! Being a person consistently motivated to take their "next step" toward Jesus is a big part of becoming a person whom others want to accompany in battle.

KNOW WHAT YOU'RE LOOKING FOR

Beyond carrying your own burdens with sincerity, you need to focus your attention on the results you're looking for. Remember, you can Google good options, so you don't need people to give you options. A litany of advice columns is available, but you aren't looking for people to give you advice. The purpose of Christian community is to find people to help you sift through the options and litany of advice to help you follow God, and then allow them to *join you* on your journey.

If you're on the wrong path, you'll find the wrong people. The efforts of people carrying their own burdens with sincerity in the direction of Jesus seem foreign if you're not on the same journey. Once you're on the right path, it's much easier to accept the counsel of those headed the same direction as you.

FIND PARTNERS HEADED IN THE SAME DIRECTION

As I said before, the Christian community described in Acts and experienced by triumphant Christians today isn't something you "sign up" to experience. Man, how I wish that were the case! On the other hand, those programs offered at a local church can be a great place to discover and develop relationships with people headed the same direction as you.

Once you tackle your own spiritual journey with sincerity, you'll know what you're looking for in partners on your journey. So set out on an intentional search for instrumental relationships with people with whom you can share your burdens, sift through the options, and engage the enemy in battle.

PARTNERSHIPS ARE BIDIRECTIONAL IN NATURE

When two people or organizations enter a partnership, it's not a relationship that is only beneficial to one side or the other. It's a mutually beneficial relationship—both parties benefit in good times . . . and in bad. Treaties are very similar. Treaties are much more than peace-time agreements. A treaty is a "formal agreement between two or more states in reference to peace, alliance [in conflict], commerce, or other international relations."[101] While that definition relates to matters of state, a vital piece of partnership applies to our following Jesus. Dan Allender says, "Find like-hearted kings living in the same direction. Sign treaties. When they're at war, you're at war."[102] We are designed to need people on our journey, but not just anyone. We need like-hearted people with the same motives and destination as ours, and we need to face all of life together because it's not just about our journey. We benefit not only from their encouragement in our difficult circumstances but also from being a vital part of theirs.

You are a king. Not in the governmental sense, but far more significantly. In a personal sense, your kingdom is the range of your effective will. As a king, you reign over all that God gives you charge: your possessions, your job, your family.

Ken Davis tells of a vacation story about a trip in the family station wagon. His children were in the backseat arguing over where to sit. In other words, they were arguing over the boundaries of their kingdom. The king of those smaller kingdoms was Dad, but he was driving and the kids arguing in the backseat were out of his reach. Turning around and reaching to bring them back into his reign, he realized they were just out of the reach of his swinging arm. But a sharp tap on the brakes brought them back into play.[103] Thy kingdom come!

Treaties are a bidirectional partnership, not a one-sided agreement. When a nation signs a treaty with another nation, they partner in peace, but they also partner *as allies* in conflict. Biblical community is a mutually beneficial relationship where people of God lock arms and do life together, both in peace and conflict.

Sheila and I have been deeply blessed to have those people in our lives. It hasn't always been easy. In fact, like any relationship, at times it's very hard work. But these relationships have helped us navigate very difficult times as we follow Christ.

Thinking back to when our girls were little, we were blessed with that kind of community within a community group at our church. As we shared similar life stages with them and wanted the same "next step" relationship with Jesus, we were encouraged and challenged. We didn't share the same relational connection with every person in our group, but every person shared equally in our journey.

At times, peers offered us those relationships, and at other times we received this relationship through mentoring authority. After my wife and I got married, a senior pastor and his wife invested in us, cared for us, and challenged us to keep pressing forward. Their relational influence in our lives continues today.

When Journey Church celebrated its tenth anniversary, I was reminded of the myriad of relational influences of people who attend our church. These aren't just people whom we influence, they're also people invested in us. All these people signed treaties with us. When we were at peace, they were there. When our lives seemed like they were at war, they faced those challenges with us.

I remember when we faced a significant challenge in our little world. After more than twenty years in marriage and ministry together, Sheila had come to a dark place in her life. She was exhausted with being a pastor's wife. She was crumbling under the feeling that people expected things of her that she couldn't meet. In short, she was burnt out. She summarized that sentiment to me in these words: "I'm not sure how much longer I can do this."

We had pledged early in our marriage that we were going to stay married for better or worse, and since divorce wasn't an option, we simply wouldn't use the D-word. That night, when she said, "I don't know how much longer I can do this," I panicked. I assumed she had meant staying married to me. I was surprised she had meant she didn't know how much longer she could partner with me in ministry![104]

Here's my point: I am so thankful we had invested in relationships with close friends walking the same path. Because of fellow believers who provided encouragement to seek counseling and church leaders who were willing to give us an entire month away from ministry (not to mention those who partnered with us in prayer), Sheila and I were able to re-settle our calling, and we weathered that storm . . . together.

You might be tempted to say, "Well, it's easier for you to develop those kinds of relationships. After all, you're a pastor." But that's just not true. Pastors have the same challenges you have. Our kids have games, jobs, and homework too. Our schedules pile up with the same overload at work, expectations of people, and family obligations. We have the added internal pressure of the enemy telling us we need perfect lives to lead people. It's often hard to trust people. Living an isolated life would be much easier. It would be easier, *but it would not be better.*

Jesus, you created me in relationship and for relationship both with you and with other people around me. All too often, I try to do life on my own, errantly thinking I can do it without help. Please help me to find the courage to risk exposure in relationships with people who are headed the same direction as I am. Amen.

THE JOURNEY IS THE DESTINATION

Eternity is now in session.[105]

— John Ortberg

It's easy to oversimplify things. There's a part of all of us that just wants to fast forward past all the tension and journey language and ask for the bullet-point summary of what's expected of us. That's where our oversimplifying the gospel winds up less like a relationship that we were created to have and more like an arrangement we've made with God to make sure we go to heaven. It's where our behavior becomes more about jumping through hoops to make God happy rather than looking at our behavior as an honest way to honor God. When we oversimplify things, we tend to get the summary correct but lose all the pieces that offer us the rich and satisfying life we were intended to have.

Think of it this way: my oldest daughter, Marissa, is a registered dental assistant. She completed the education needed to assist the dentist. Marissa can look at a dental x-ray and identify a cavity. She knows which medication will be used to numb someone's mouth, which instruments will be used to drill out the area, and what material will be used to fill the cavity. I trust Marissa a great deal, but I wouldn't feel comfortable with her drilling out and filling a cavity in my mouth. Why? I don't have confidence in her education, experience, and perspective. It's perfectly fine to assist the dentist, but much of the vital pieces have been simplified to help her effectively assist the dentist.

The same thing happens when we oversimplify the whole gospel to only being sure we go to heaven and making a list of things to do and not to do. We run a grave danger of completely missing the most important parts of who God wants us to *become* along the journey. We need to focus less on the bullet-point summary of what's expected and more on the journey with Jesus itself. The journey of becoming *with* Jesus is the destination he intended for us. My intention for you in this book has been to introduce you to the more that you were intended to live—a way to find the rich and satisfying life Jesus promised.

There is no magic solution or combination of words and actions that will unlock the life that's promised. It is, instead, a life of discovery, adventure, and trust—a journey with Jesus rather than a destination of heaven.

In these pages, I've introduced you to two critical principles. First, God wants more for your life than just going to heaven when you die. There are dangers to oversimplifying the message that Jesus came to bring. He came to bring the kingdom of God to earth.

> THERE IS MORE OFFERED TO YOU IN PURSUIT OF THE RICH AND SATISFYING LIFE THAT GOD HAS FOR YOU—IT'S MORE THAN JUST MAKING SURE YOU GO TO HEAVEN WHEN YOU DIE.

The great news is that you and Jesus want the same for your life: more! You were never intended *just to believe* the right information about him and mind your manners until you go to heaven. Don't miss the value of believing the right information, and please know that your behavior does matter, but that's not the end of the story. Pushing the more that you were made for is what this life is all about.

Second, the parts of your journey are interconnected. Like gears, they must all work in unison. One cannot grind to a halt without slowing (or stopping) the others. Together, these five critical areas of your life contain the journey you're intended to walk *with* Jesus—a journey of identity, intimacy, truth, authenticity, and community. Hopefully, by now you've realized that what we've done in these pages is simply open the box and peek inside. Each of these categories contains a lifetime of journey *with* Jesus to explore. It's now yours to walk in, explore, and experience with Jesus—and to pass on.

JESUS CAME TO SAVE THE LOST

Matthew and Luke both record a very important parable that Jesus told. I can only imagine its importance to them was tied to their own story—one of rescue. It's encompassed in just a small handful of verses, but the meaning and value for us is nothing short of profound.

> If a man has a hundred sheep and one of them wanders away, what will he do? Won't he leave the ninety-nine others on the hills and go out to search for the one that is lost? And if he finds it, I tell you the truth, he will rejoice over it more than over the ninety-nine that didn't wander

157

away! In the same way, it is not my heavenly Father's will that even one of these little ones should perish.[106]

The idea seems ludicrous, doesn't it? A shepherd's leaving the ninety-nine sheep to chase after the lost one? It doesn't make sense to us because we see only the ratio of safe sheep to lost sheep. For us, leaving the ninety-nine at risk to chase after the one doesn't seem like a wise calculation. But what we're missing is the value that Jesus places on the one. Just a few chapters after Luke shares this same parable, he records Jesus' own words describing exactly what he came to do:

> For the Son of Man came to seek and save those who are lost.[107]

We covered this verse in another context, but let's walk through its value again here. Jesus came for one reason: to seek and save the lost. He deeply loves his children, and his sacrifice for them demonstrates that he's willing to go to any means necessary to redeem us. In fact, Peter records this statement about God's willingness to express his love for his children:

> The Lord isn't really being slow about his promise, as some people think. No, he is being patient for your sake. He does not want anyone to be destroyed, but wants everyone to repent.[108]

Last words are important words. When someone is leaving this world and makes the effort to say one last thing, everyone present leans in with expectation. When Jesus left this world to go to the Father, he left us with one final statement called the Great

Commission. Jesus challenged us to take this whole message to the lost sheep that he placed in our lives to reach.

> Therefore, go and make disciples of all the nations, baptizing them in the name of the Father and the Son and the Holy Spirit. Teach these new disciples to obey all the commands I have given you. And be sure of this: I am with you always, even to the end of the age.[109]

This message is not just about your own redemption story. Part of why God redeemed you is to put you on mission with him—to prick your heart with compassion for the one who is still lost. Earlier in the book, I talked about what a disciple looks like: a disciple is a person who is a follower of Jesus who is formed in the image of Jesus and faithful to the mission of Jesus. If you want to err on the side of behavior, be about the mission that Jesus left for us to accomplish. The mission of developing a heart for the lost and going to whatever means necessary to reach them.

Who do you know needs to hear about the more that they were created for?

Who do you know still needs to hear of the rich and satisfying life available to them?

Who do you know needs to know their past no longer has to define them?

Who do you know is living a meaningless existence apart from a loving relationship with the God who created them?

Who do you know needs to live in healing rather than hurt?

Who do you know needs to have a lens of truth with which to see the world?

Who do you know needs to find deep and meaningful community that will encourage them?

Who do you know needs Jesus and the life he offers?

Well, now it's your turn to make a move toward them. Invest this message in your story, and then invite them to join you for the more you were both created for. It is, after all, Jesus' last words of commission to you: go and make disciples. It is what disciples do.

NOTES

2. John 10:10.

3. Greg Lindsey, lead pastor at Discovery Church in Colorado Springs, CO, used this phrase in a sermon. You can listen to Greg at www.livetorescue.com.

4. John Ortberg, *Eternity Is Now in Session: A Radical Rediscovery of What Jesus Really Taught About Salvation, Eternity, and Getting to the Good Place* (Carol Stream, IL: Tyndale, 2018), 5.

5. cf. Matthew 25:23.

6. Matt Chandler, *The Explicit Gospel* (Wheaton, IL: Crossway, 2012), 481.

7. cf. Matthew 23:25; Luke 11:39.

8. cf. 2 Timothy 2:12; Revelation 20:4–6.

9. Gary Black, *Preparing for Heaven* (New York: HarperOne, 2015), 22.

10. John Piper, *Future Grace: The Purifying Power of the Promises of God,* rev. ed. (Colorado Springs: Multnomah Books, 2012), 144.

11. cf. Matthew 4:19, ESV.

12. John Ortberg, *"God Is Closer Than You Think* Quotes," Goodreads, accessed March 19, 2021, https://www.goodreads.com/work/quotes/213781.

13. C. S. Lewis, *The Complete C. S. Lewis Signature Classics* (San Francisco: HarperOne, 2002), 155.

14. I heard John Eldredge say this at a *Wild At Heart* boot camp in February 2016.

15. cf. 1 Timothy 6:15; Revelation 17:14.

16. You can watch Makayla falling for the blinker fluid trick here: Jeremy Brown, "Blink Fluid," YouTube video, 0:32, September 20, 2021, https://www.youtube.com/watch?v=bbq4Bl73m_Y.

17. Matthew 28:19, NIV, emphasis mine.

18. Several other groups (e.g., Mormons and Jehovah's Witnesses) believe that Jesus is *a* god or that Jesus *became* God, but they don't believe Jesus *is* God. These are examples of people who name Jesus by name, but they don't believe in the Jesus of the Scriptures.

19. Luke 19:10.

20. Jesus used the words "Son of Man" thirty times in Matthew, fourteen times in Mark, twenty-five times in Luke, and twelve times in John.

21. Genesis 2:17.

22. This quote is famously attributed to A. W. Tozer. It was likely used in a sermon, but I can't find the original context.

23. Ortberg, *Eternity Is Now in Session*, 35.

24. Matthew 23:27–28.

25. Ephesians 1:5.

26. Ephesians 1:1.

27. 2 Corinthians 5:21.

28. Ginny Owens, "Made for More," track five on *I Know a Secret,* Chick Power Music, 2015, compact disc.

29. cf. Isaiah 61:1.

30. NIV.

31. Ronald Heifetz, "The Nature of Adaptive Leadership," YouTube video, 8:59, Faith and Leadership, February 4, 2009, accessed October 18, 2020, http://www.youtube.com/watch?v=QfLLDvn0pI8.%E2%80%9D.

32. Matthew 4:19, NIV.

33. cf. Ephesians 5:18.

34. cf. Romans 3:23.

35. Alan Cross, "Where Did the Phrase 'Sex, Drugs, and Rock'n'Roll' Actually Come from?" *A Journal of Musical Things* (blog), April 6, 2016, https://www.ajournalofmusicalthings.com/phrase-sex-drugs-rocknroll-actually-come/.

36. Haggai 1:8.

37. NIV.

38. Luke 4:18–19.

39. cf. Luke 4:21.

40. cf. Isaiah 61:1; Luke 4:18.

41. In an effort to give credit where credit is due, I got almost all of this from conversations with Stuart Hall. You can follow him on social media, or just become his friend after sending him an email accusing him of highway robbery. That's what I did.

42. Morgan Snyder, *Becoming a King: The Path to Restoring the Heart of a Man* (Nashville: Thomas Nelson, 2020), 81.

43. *The Wedding Singer*, directed by Frank Coraci (1998; Burbank: New Line Cinema), film.

44. I'm sure I didn't come up with these pyramids, but I can't figure out where they came from. It may either be a resource I can no longer remember or a conglomeration of resources over the years. Either way, I don't claim credit.

45. Hebrews 5:12.

46. Neil T. Anderson, *Victory over the Darkness* (Bloomington, MN: Bethany House, 2013), 118.

47. Genesis 3:7.

48. Genesis 3:8–10.

49. Genesis 3:11–12.

50. Ephesians 2:10.

51. Matthew 6:25–26.

52. Ephesians 2:18.

53. Ephesians 1:5.

54. Ephesians 2:18.

55. Romans 8:1.

56. Romans 8:28.

57. Romans 8:35ff.

58. 2 Timothy 1:7.

59. Matthew 5:13.

60. Matthew 5:14.

61. Matthew 5:16.

62. John 15:4.

63. Philippians 1:6.

64. 1 Corinthians 3:16.

65. 2 Corinthians 6:1.

66. Philippians 4:13.

67. Snyder, 18.

68. Mark 1:15.

69. cf. Luke 8:1; Luke 9:27; Acts 1:3.

70. John Ortberg, "Why Heaven Is a Lot Closer Than You Think," *Outreach Magazine,* November 18, 2018, https://outreachmagazine.com/resources/books/theology/37288-why-heaven-is-a-lot-closer-than-you-think.html.

71. Matthew 6:33, ESV.

Notes

72. Dallas Willard, *The Divine Conspiracy: Rediscovering Our Hidden Life in God* (San Francisco: HarperCollins, 1998), 21–22, Kindle.

73. Colossians 1:17, NIV.

74. Matthew 8:8–9.

75. Craig Groeschel, Twitter post, March 4, 2020, 8:00 a.m., https://twitter.com/craiggroeschel/status/107935542 5361936385?lang=en.

76. John 15:4–5, ESV.

77. In talking with those in charge of shepherding the works of Dallas Willard, I was not able to nail down the specific place where Dallas said these words, although they certainly resound with his teachings.

78. 2 Timothy 3:16–17, ESV.

79. Steve Porter, "The Willardian Corpus," *Journal of Spiritual Formation & Soul Care* 3, no. 2 (2010): 245, http://media. biola.edu/pdf/SFJ-Willard.pdf.

80. Snyder, 18.

81. Porter, ibid.

82. Very broadly, there are at least two camps of Christ followers when it comes to how God speaks to his people. One believes God stopped speaking outside of the words of Scripture to his people (cessationism). The other holds that God still speaks to and works through his children today (continuationism). As in most issues, I believe the truth lies somewhere in the middle. It's a logical fallacy to set up a black-and-white option and dismiss another potential perspective. Therefore, I'm a radical moderate—certainly abuses and inconsistencies are on both sides. I can't choose a perspective that limits how God chooses

to work. God still speaks to us today within the boundaries of his Word.

83. John 10:3.

84. There are multiple resources related to hearing God's voice. To be honest, you can get yourself into some risky places with some of them. After you've established a solid foundation in the written Word of God, here are two resources that offer a trustworthy perspective: John Eldredge, *Walking with God: How to Hear His Voice* (Nashville: Thomas Nelson, 2016) and Dallas Willard, *Hearing God: Developing a Conversation with God* (Downers Grove, IL: IVP, 2012).

85. I'm indebted to John Eldredge for shaping this process in my mind. While this process isn't outlined in one place (that I know of), it's certainly at least an amalgam of his teaching in various places.

86. Ephesians 6:10–12.

87. Ephesians 6:13–18.

88. Snyder, 17.

89. Al Franken, "Stuart Smalley — Daily Affirmations," *SNL*, YouTube video, 0:47, uploaded February 22, 2011, https://www.youtube.com/watch?v=6ldAQ6Rh5ZI.

90. Jeremiah 17:9, NIV.

91. John Eldredge, *Wild at Heart: Discovering the Secret of a Man's Soul* (Nashville: Thomas Nelson, 2001, 145).

92. cf. 1 Peter 5:8; John 8:44; John 10:10; John 10:28–30.

93. I've had the privilege over the last five years of being healed of my personal wounds by reading, listening to, and watching videos by John Eldredge and Dan Allender. While you could likely watch just about any of them and yield great benefit, you might start by reading some of these resources. Men might

start with *Wild at Heart* by John Eldredge. Ladies might like the companion book *Captivating* (Nashville: Thomas Nelson, 2011), which his wife, Stasi, wrote. Dan Allender has written numerous books, and many of them deal with healing emotional wounds. You might start with *The Healing Path: How the Hurts in Your Past Can Lead You to a More Abundant Life* (Colorado Springs: Multnomah Books, 2000).

94. Luke 4:13, NIV.

95. Malcolm Gladwell, *Outliers: The Story of Success* (Boston: Back Bay Books, 2011), 47.

96. Genesis 2:18, NIV, emphasis mine.

97. The words "helper alongside" are an English translation of the Hebrew words *ēzer neḡeḏ* used in Genesis 2:18 and translated in the NIV as "helper suitable for him."

98. Acts 2:42–44, 46, NIV.

99. Snyder, 167.

100. *Gladiator,* directed by Ridley Scott (2000, Universal City: Dreamworks Pictures), film.

101. *Dictionary.com*, s.v. "treaty," accessed on March 18, 2021, https://www.dictionary.com/browse/treaty.

102. Snyder, ibid.

103. Ken Davis, "Unruly Kids in the Car," YouTube video, 2:09, January 17, 2016, https://youtu.be/ALKd6BzmfR0.

104. You can listen to Sheila's story in a podcast she did for Stadia's Bloom Ministry (a ministry for women in church planting): https://podcasts.apple.com/us/podcast/sheila-brown-on-celebrating-10-years-of-church-planting/id1370090355?i=1000491438920. Or you can read her chapter, "Believing the Lies," in *Named+Known: Uncovering the*

Identities of Women Who Plant Churches, ed. Heidy Tandy (self-pub., 2019).

105. Ortberg, *Eternity Is Now in Session*, 6.
106. Matthew 18:12–14.
107. Luke 19:10.
108. 2 Peter 3:9.
109. Matthew 28:19–20.

ABOUT THE AUTHOR

JEREMY BROWN has been married to his wife, Sheila, for just over twenty-five years. Together, they have three wonderful girls, Marissa, Makayla, and Myah (and a wonderful son-in-law, Collin). After both graduating from Moody Bible Institute, Jeremy and Sheila have served the church for all their married lives. Jeremy served eighteen years in student ministry and for the past eleven years as the lead pastor at Journey Church near Jackson, Tennessee (the church he and Shelia planted through a partnership with Stadia).

Jeremy loves great conversations and friendship (usually over great cigars) and likes to play golf. He's passionate about helping people take their "next step" toward Jesus, which is the mission of the church he leads today.